MW01491282

GUIDE TO YOUR
VIVID
JOURNEY

About Jessica Alaire

Jessica is a Midwest native who likes to express herself with flowing lines and vivid colors. Always feeling a close relationship with nature and the flowing energies around her, she strives to capture that in her art. As a self-taught artist, Jessica always viewed her art as an extension of herself, her soul brought to life, and the best way to express her feelings and spirituality. Now she wants to share her art with the world in hopes that her work will brighten the lives of those it touches. Still a student of tarot, Jessica wanted to create a tarot deck based around color that used the elements she learned from her few years of study, to further her own understanding and to help others learn the beautiful art of tarot card reading.

To Write to the Author

If you wish to contact the author or would like more information about this book, please write to the author in care of Llewellyn Worldwide, and we will forward your request. Please write to:

Jessica Alaire
℅ Llewellyn Worldwide
2143 Wooddale Drive
Woodbury, MN 55125-2989

Please enclose a self-addressed stamped envelope for reply, or $1.00 to cover costs. If outside the USA, enclose an international postal reply coupon.

GUIDE TO YOUR
VIVID
JOURNEY

JESSICA ALAIRE

Llewellyn Worldwide
Woodbury, Minnesota

First Edition
First Printing, 2017

Book design by Bob Gaul
Cover and card art by Jessica Alaire
Cover design by Ellen Lawson
Interior card spread by Llewellyn art department

Llewellyn Publications is a registered trademark of Llewellyn Worldwide Ltd.

Library of Congress Cataloging-in-Publication Data
ISBN: 978-0-7387-5071-2

The Vivid Journey Tarot consists of a boxed set of 78 full-color cards
and this perfect bound book.

Llewellyn Worldwide Ltd. does not participate in, endorse, or have any authority or responsibility concerning private business transactions between our authors and the public.

All mail addressed to the author is forwarded, but the publisher cannot, unless specifically instructed by the author, give out an address or phone number.

Any Internet references contained in this work are current at publication time, but the publisher cannot guarantee that a specific location will continue to be maintained. Please refer to the publisher's website for links to authors' websites and other sources.

Llewellyn Publications
A Division of Llewellyn Worldwide Ltd.
2143 Wooddale Drive
Woodbury, MN 55125-2989
www.llewellyn.com

Printed in China

CONTENTS

Introduction

Welcome to the fun, intriguing, introspective spiritual journey of tarot. Following closely in the traditions of the Rider-Waite-Smith methodology, the Vivid Journey uses flowing lines and striking, coordinating colors to illustrate an illuminated visual journey for you to interpret. Color is a very powerful tool, interacting with its viewer to create vivid moods, emotions, and thoughts. The *Vivid Journey Tarot* seeks to harness that power to evoke intuitive responses to the question at hand, while still complementing the original symbolism. Whether you are a tarot novice or a seasoned veteran, this deck was designed for everyone.

Tarot is a journey, following the Fool along the pathway through the major arcana and the metaphorical journey of life. My personal journey with tarot started at a very young age but wasn't truly awakened until a few years ago. I had always been fascinated with tarot and the occult but from an uninformed perspective—that tarot was a dark, mystical art only usable by a select few. I pictured late-night TV psychics telling fortunes and predicting the future. The bright colors, interesting images, and symbolism of tarot always intrigued me, but I didn't think I had the "gift" to read and truly understand the cards. After discovering that a good friend was a long-time tarot reader and picking her brain to the point of annoyance, I learned that everything I thought I knew about tarot was a misconception. Tarot isn't dark or evil. It is simply a tool you use to tap into your intuition and inner guides. The cards themselves are not empowered with any mystical power; rather they are a key that helps us unlock our own inner link to the divine. Tarot taps into those inner "gut" feelings, intuitions, and inner guides that we all have but often ignore. The small, static images illuminate our innermost predicaments and desires. Anyone can read tarot. With a little time and practice, you too can understand the world of tarot.

After my eyes were opened to the true wonder of tarot, I read as many books as I could get my hands on. I bought my very first deck, a Rider-Waite, and studied it constantly. However, no matter how much I tried or how much I memorized the meanings of each card, I struggled to connect on a truly deep level. While I love and respect that deck tremendously, the images weren't giving me the flow I so desperately wanted. After searching through other beautiful tarot decks but still not finding something that really clicked with me, I thought it would be best if I just made my own. I have always used art and painting to express my feelings and to put my personal energies into the world. During the year-and-a-half-long creation process and after some feedback from my friends who knew nothing about tarot, the purpose for my deck changed. It went from simply being a personal learning process to something I wanted to use to help others learn about the amazing world of tarot cards. I wanted to take the traditional symbolism and really meld in the emotional power of color to create a deck that truly resonates with each reader individually. I wanted a deck that could help people who knew nothing of tarot learn to read, but I also wanted a deck that held true to the Rider-Waite-Smith symbolism that would make even the most seasoned tarot masters happy. I am not a master of tarot myself by any definition of the term—I'm very much still a student—but I want to share the tips and tricks that really helped me along my tarot path to get a deeper understanding of the cards.

I am the first person to admit that creating seventy-eight individual works of art is a very daunting task and not for everyone, so don't feel like you must create your own deck to really learn. That is a big part of why I crafted this deck, to serve as a good starting point for *you* to dive into tarot. The Vivid Journey will help you develop a solid base knowledge you can then take with you and explore other decks. You can become like the vast majority of tarot readers who quickly become tarot collectors. Like myself and nearly every tarot reader I've talked to, you'll soon have at least a handful of favorite decks you read depending on your mood, season, or purpose. Before we start collecting, let's start with a little tarot history.

ONE

~

TAROT BASICS

Tarot originated in the mid-fifteenth century, throughout Europe, as a card game. It wasn't until the eighteenth century that tarot began being used as a tool for divination. A French freemason and Protestant pastor named Antoine Court de Gébelin is believed to be the first person to attribute hidden meanings to tarot for the means of divination. There are many versions of tarot decks, many of which are still used to this day. Tarot of Marseilles, the Rider-Waite-Smith deck, and the Thoth tarot are the three most popular decks that have become the systems after which most modern decks are modeled. The Vivid Journey follows the Rider-Waite-Smith system. Any descriptions herein pertain only to that style of deck and the Vivid Journey tarot specifically. Now let's break down the basics of the tarot deck.

The deck itself is made up of seventy-eight cards divided into two groups: the major arcana and the minor arcana. The major arcana is made up of the twenty-two trump cards.

The minor arcana is made up of four different suits: cups, wands, swords, and pentacles. Each suit is then further made up of the four court cards and ten pip (numbered) cards. The pip cards are ace through ten, and the court cards are king, queen, knight, and page. Every card in the deck uses small scenic images to represent an archetype. As described by Carl Jung, an archetype is "a pattern of thought that is universally present in all human psyches." Everyone can gain insight through tarot because it uses the fundamental building blocks we all share. We will get more into the breakdown of the archetypes later. First, we will discuss my favorite part of this deck: color.

Color is a very powerful tool that shapes how we see and interpret the world around us. It has been scientifically proven that color can change our emotional state. Blues are very calming, while shades of bright red are stimulating and can evoke anger or fear. Think about how horror movies use vivid splashes of red to arouse feelings of unease in the audience. The use of color in tarot is no different; color makes us *feel* the cards, helping us easily tap into our subconscious connection with the universe and the energies around us. This deck's vivid colors will hopefully help you get a better connection to your inner guides and to the guidance that you seek. Here is a little color symbolism:

- **Red**: Red is the color that pumps through our veins. It is primal. Red brings us messages of aggression, passion, power, lust, action, danger, and desire.

- **Orange**: Orange is the harmony between powerful red and bright yellow. It is fun, playful, healing, warm, and comforting.

- **Yellow**: Yellow is light and bright. The color of the sun, yellow is vitality, healing, positivity, creativity, illumination, and clarity.

- **Green**: Green is the soothing blend of bright yellow and calming blue. Green is the predominant color of nature. It is youth, growth, money, prosperity, and health.

- **Blue**: Blue is as vast as the sky and as deep as the ocean. It is calming, tranquil, open, and free. It is also is emotional, inspirational, and sensitive.

- **Violet**: Violet is the perfect marriage of passionate red and tranquil blue. Violet is problem solving, intuitive, resurrection, and the psychic realm. Violet is also associated with royalty and grandeur.

- **Brown**: Brown is the color of soil. It is earthy, grounding, stable, solid, and serious.

- **Black:** Black is all colors mixed together. It is the void, darkness, the end, a culmination of things, formality, convention, and stability.

- **White**: White is the absence of color. It is purity, beginning, cleansing, innocence, and faith. White illuminates the darkness.

Now that we have discussed the importance of color and before getting into the individual cards, I want to share with you a tip that helped me tremendously with my understanding of the cards: keep a tarot journal and practice with daily one-card readings. I started my readings by grounding myself and clearing my mind, taking notes on how I felt emotionally before and after the reading. I would focus on asking the universe what I needed to understand or clarify on that day. I would shuffle and cut the deck as I focused. Once I felt ready, I would draw one card. I would then really try to feel what that card was trying to show me. I would jot down key words and feelings I attached to that card. Only after I tried to feel the card intuitively and got stuck would I look up the meaning. I would then continue to take notes and decipher what the card was trying to tell me about the day. With a little time and practice it becomes a lot easier to read the cards, and you'll have to look up the given meanings less and less.

It is very important to remember that tarot is personal. What works for you isn't going to work for everyone else. There is no right or wrong way to read tarot cards. You don't have to shuffle them a certain way or even lay them out in a certain way; you must only do what feels right to you. This is about tapping into your intuition and inner divine connection. If the given meaning of a card doesn't match what you see in the card, go with your gut! This is about what you see and feel, not what a book is telling you to see and feel. I want you to take these tarot fundamentals and mold them to work for you.

After you feel comfortable with a single card, you can move onto full tarot spreads.

A tarot spread is the actual card layout for the reading. There are simple spreads and more complicated ones; you can use pre-made spreads or make your own. Each spread has a specified card placement with a meaning or significance tied to it. Confused? Me too, but don't worry, I'm about to show you an example. One of my favorite spreads, and probably one of the simplest, is the three-card spread:

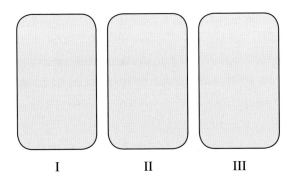

I   II   III

- To begin, clear your mind and ground yourself. Focus on a situation or question on which you would like more guidance. While you concentrate on the question or situation, begin shuffling and cutting the cards however you'd like. When you feel ready to begin, turn a card face up in the first card position. Do the same for the second and third card positions.

- The first card represents your past, specifically something or someone from your past that is affecting you now.

- The second card represents your present. This could be something or someone that is playing a large role in your situation.

- The third card represents your future. This is something that can flow out of your current situation if you stay on your current path.

Now that you know the positions, I want you to read the cards exactly like you did the one card reading. Focus or meditate with the cards and try to understand them intuitively—only look up the given card meaning if you get stuck. Look at how the cards are flowing into one another. Which direction are the characters in the cards facing? What could that be trying to tell you? Are any of the cards reversed (upside down)? You don't have to read reversals, but if you do, a good rule of thumb to remember is that reversals signify the opposite meaning of the card or that the meaning is being blocked by something. If you don't want to read reversals, simply place the card right side up as you lay them out and read as you would normally.

What colors do you see? How do those colors make you feel? What details were your eyes drawn to first? Do the numbers on the card signify anything to you? What is the story these cards are trying to show you? Also keep in mind that we often let our wants and desires cloud what is actually happening in our lives. Your intuitive voice isn't that screaming loud voice inside, it's that calm and whispering voice. It is that voice you just *know* is correct even if it is saying what you don't want to hear, and it is the place the cards are tapping into. There will be times when you have a reading that doesn't seem to make any sense at all; in times like this, it's a good idea to take notes or keep a tarot journal. I have found many times that my true understanding of a reading didn't come until much later after certain events had transpired. It's nice to be able to validate old readings that confused you at the time.

Remember: you can change the meanings of a spread if it doesn't suit you. The "past/present/future" three-card spread is probably the most popular, but I also like the "situation/action/outcome" and "situation/problem/resolution" three-card spreads. Feel free to do whatever you want. You can add cards, change the meanings, lay cards in a fun shape, or whatever else comes to mind. The only guidance I will give here is to make sure you set in stone what your spread is before you begin the actual reading. If you change the meanings in the middle of a reading, you won't get an accurate reading because you aren't staying true to the energy you put forth when you started it. After you get more comfortable reading yourself or if you are struggling to read yourself, you can practice reading your friends. Reading for other people works the same way as reading for yourself, only their energy is also flowing through the cards. You'll want to have them also clear their mind and focus on the situation in question, and they'll need to cut or shuffle the cards (if possible). Don't get discouraged if you have trouble reading yourself or other people. It is often harder to read ourselves because we are too emotionally invested and too focused on what we want to happen. It takes a lot of time and practice. No one is good at this right out of the gate; don't be discouraged. Now that we've got the intuitive basics down, let's start breaking down the given meanings of the cards themselves.

Let's begin with the major arcana. These are the twenty-two trump cards (that is, the Fool numbered 0 and the twenty-one trump cards. The major arcana tell a story of the Fool's journey through life. The Fool represents the human psyche, and this is where the archetypes come into play. Each major arcana card represents one of the main human archetypes. The Fool's journey is a metaphor for life's path. The innocent Fool begins her journey naively moving without any regard for the environment and energies around her. She is spontaneous and a blank slate, much like a newborn. Immediately after setting off on her journey the Fool runs into the Magician. The Magician represents our conscious mind. He is masculine and active. Immediately across from the Magician sits his opposite, the High Priestess. She represents our unconscious mind. She is our hidden potential, strong yet patiently waiting. After the High Priestess, the Fool recognizes her mother, the Empress. She represents nurturing and fertility. Opposite her is the Emperor; the Fool's father. The Emperor represents structure and authority. After her parents, the Fool encounters the Hierophant. He is the educator and priest. He represents the belief system we all develop as we learn about the world around us. As the Fool begins to feel the lustful urges of young adulthood, she happens upon the Lovers. They represent more than that, however; they also show the balance of a meaningful relationship and partnership. As the Fool continues into adulthood, she encounters the Chariot. The Chariot represents strong physical self-control. With a youthful confidence and assertive nature, the Chariot rides proudly. However, with confidence often comes over-confidence, and here the Fool finds herself with a prideful beast. Thankfully, Strength comes in to help. She shows a gentler way to tackle her problems via inner strength. Strength uses nurturing and patience to tame the wild beast. After taming the beast, the Fool comes across the Hermit. He represents the search for life's deeper meaning. The Fool turns inward using times of solitude and meditation to discover what makes us all tick. After some self-exploration she happens upon the Wheel of Fortune. The Wheel represents the universe's cyclical nature, and it is about motion and destiny. Now that the Fool is starting to see her small role in the grand design, she encounters Justice. With her scales, Justice is about answering to your actions. She represents balance and karma. She shows the Fool that she must take responsibility for what she does. Continuing on her path, the Fool happens upon a tree with a man hanging upside down. He is the Hanged Man, a representation of sacrifice. Yet even while hanging, he has a peaceful demeanor. The Hanged Man is about letting go. Now that the Fool has begun purging herself of old habits, she happens upon Death. Death represents transitions and transformations. Not necessarily permanent, Death is about ending one stage to start anew. As the Fool begins to understand the essential changes in life she comes across Temperance, who represents balance specifically related to health and well-being. Temperance is soft and soothing. After Temperance, while continuing deeper along her path, the Fool comes face to face with the Devil. The Devil represents the ignorance and anguish that resides within all of us. He is the drive to hold on to the materialistic world. Desperately trying to free herself from the Devil, the Fool discovers The Tower. The Tower represents a radical change. It is about breaking down those walls we build to protect us; they really only hold us prisoner. It is a difficult process, but the outcome makes the pain well worth it. After breaking down the barriers, the Fool comes across the Star. She represents hope and inspiration. She is naked because she doesn't hide from the world. She is tranquil and calm. Just past the Star, the Fool sees the Moon. She represents imagination and illusion. Bubbling up from the sea below her are unconscious thoughts and ideas. However, with those thoughts are often unconscious fears and anxieties. Thankfully for the Fool, the Sun comes along and shines its light to illuminate the darkness. The Sun represents enlightenment and vitality. Thanks to the Sun, the Fool is now reenergized and beginning to understand her own greatness. Feeling almost reborn, the Fool comes upon Judgement. Judgement represents a higher calling to reach your full potential. It is about your own personal judgment day wherein you forgive yourself and others so you can move forward and become one with your higher self. Finally on her journey the Fool encounters the World. The World represents accomplishment and completion. The

Fool has traveled the path of life and ended up a happier, more self-aware person. She learned that we are all pure at our core and the basis for life is happiness. We hold happiness in ourselves but must discover it on our own path through life.

Now that we've covered the major arcana let's explore the minor arcana. The minors are broken down into four different suits: wands, cups, swords, and pentacles. The suits themselves each have a corresponding element, color, and overall meaning. I have color-coded the suits in this deck to help keep them even more cohesive.

- **Wands**: The wands are represented by the element fire, the season of summer, and the color red. They represent the actions, primal urges, and burning passions that drive us.

- **Cups**: The cups are represented by the element water, the season of autumn, and the color blue. They represent our emotional side, our desires, emotional reactions, and sensitivities.

- **Swords**: The swords are represented by the element of air, the season of spring, and the color yellow. They represent our thinking, mental selves, decision-making, and reasoning.

- **Pentacles**: The pentacles are represented by the element of earth, the season of winter, and the color green. They represent our physical selves, our health, and material possessions such as money.

Each suit contains four court cards: king, queen, knight, and page. Just like the other cards, the court cards represent archetypes. They can represent the overall stages of life, or they can convey the stages of mastering a skill. They usually signify either a part of yourself or someone else in your life.

- **Kings and Queens**: The kings and queens represent adulthood or the mastery of the skill or tool. They bring the balance of the masculine and feminine.

- **Knights**: The knights represent adolescence or the action, diligence, and hard work needed to perfect that new skill or tool.

- **Pages**: The pages represent childhood or curiosity, interest, and enthusiasm to begin a new skill or use a new tool. They are messengers, bringing news and new bits of information.

Each court card doesn't really describe physical age as much as it speaks of the mental or soul age. A king or queen could represent that young person in your life who is wise beyond their years, or a page might represent that old friend who refuses to grow up. A queen could be telling you that you need to tap into your feminine side while a king may show you that a more masculine approach is the way to go.

Each suit also contains ten pip cards, numbered ten though ace. Some prefer to order the cards in ascending order from ace to ten, but because this deck so closely follows the RWS deck I chose to keep the order A. E. Waite laid out in his original book.

Choose whichever order you personally prefer. Like each page, knight, queen, or king card, each pip of the same number has a general theme that ties them together.

- **Tens**: The tens of the deck usually represent accomplishment and completion. They show us that we have completed this cycle and are ready to celebrate, relax, and then begin the next one.

- **Nines**: The nines of the deck usually indicate that we are very close to completing our goals but aren't quite there yet. They remind us that we still have to work a little more before we are finished.

- **Eights**: The eights of the deck often speak of a rejuvenated call to action toward our goal. They represent forward movement and a positive push in the right direction.

- **Sevens**: The sevens of the deck often represent a time to focus on growing ourselves as a whole. They often suggest taking a break, meditation, introspection, expanding knowledge, and strengthening our faith.

- **Sixes**: The sixes of the deck usually indicate problem solving, communication, and overcoming the setbacks found in the fives. Sixes often represent a need to adjust our thinking or plans to get back on track.

- **Fives**: The fives of the deck are sometimes seen as the opposite of the overall feeling of the suit. They are generally seen as a speed bump or hurdle in the process of realizing our goals.

- **Fours**: The fours of the deck grow on the energy and hard work in the previous numbers and show us the importance of establishing a firm foundation and building from there. They also represent starting to see results from all of your work.

- **Threes**: The threes of the deck often speak of taking the decisions and energy of the previous cards and growing our plans into reality. These cards show growth and community—development in our plans and working together with others to better reach our goals.

- **Twos**: The twos of the deck are usually indicative of keeping balance, making a choice between two equally weighted options, or coming to a crossroads.

- **Aces**: The aces of the deck are the purest form of the energy each suit emanates. They represent new beginnings, and inspiration, and are often a sign to start a new project and move forward with any plans.

It is very important to remember that tarot isn't a substitute for a doctor or certified professional when the situation calls for one. If you are reading others, you must remember that a reading is confidential. You shouldn't share any part of a reading with anyone else. As the reader you are being entrusted with personal information and, in a way, shown a window into the other person's core. This great privilege should only be met with a high level of respect and care.

I want to stress one last time before we go through each individual card that tarot is personal. If you completely disagree with a given meaning of a card, write in your own meaning. The following meanings are simply how I like to interpret the cards. The only *true* meanings are the ones your intuition tells you are correct. Make them your own. Take notes in a journal or even within the margins of this book. Keeping a journal helps keep all of your tarot workings in one place. If you don't like reversals, don't use them. Every card has a balance of positive and negative meanings. Use your gut to incorporate whichever meaning you feel best suits your reading. If the King of Cups reminds you of your favorite uncle, jot down some of his characteristics. If the Nine of Pentacles is the spitting image of your crazy neighbor, write it in. Your intuition is telling you these things for a reason, and reading is all about what the cards mean to you; no one can tell you otherwise. On its own, tarot isn't that powerful; it is merely a tool. It allows you to tap into your own inner power and connection to the divine. It will only work if you make it your own and infuse your energy into every bit of it.

TWO

~

MAJOR ARCANA

Following are the twenty-two major arcana, the Fool through the World, 0 through XXI.

Are you ready to go on your journey?

0 · THE FOOL

The Fool is unafraid to begin her journey. She pays no mind to the dangers ahead of her because she holds her faith deeply. I drew her nude and in silhouette to convey the blank slate and innocence we all possess at the beginning of our journey. The white rose in her hand also conveys her purity. Surrounded by a vibrant yellow sun, she is full of vitality and unlimited potential. Her dog is her guide, warning her of the dangerous cliff ahead. He is there to help her learn the lessons the path of life has for her, reminding her to not rush things. The Fool speaks to us of beginnings and starting fresh. She tells us to follow our hearts. Like the Fool, we must move forward with confidence and take that "leap of faith" even though we have no idea what the future holds for us. The Fool is a very good meditation card to get clarity on how we are being perceived and how we perceive the world. She reminds us to trust the process, and the dog brings balance to show that we still need to pay attention to what is happening around us.

If the Fool comes up reversed, she shows us that we are not in that balance. She might be trying to tell us that we are taking carefree nature to its negative extreme. Are you acting recklessly? Are you moving forward with absolutely no regard for others? Are you doing yourself or others harm because of that disregard? The Fool reversed reminds us that there are consequences to our actions. She also tells us that we need to realize those full consequences before jumping into any new deals or opportunities. Faith is a wonderful thing, but blind faith can have very serious repercussions. If we remember this when faced with future decisions, we can make changes today to regain balance.

1 · THE MAGICIAN

The Magician represents our conscious mind and control. He is a
very masculine card. He shows us that we are in ultimate control
of our conscious mind and therefore our own realities. The deep
red of his cloak represents that power and control. The four suits
marked on his cloak represent the four elements. The Magician

is the master of those elements. The vibrant yellow behind him represents the illumination and clarity we all possess. This card is all about realizing your full potential. It shows us that we are born with the ability and power to take action and move ourselves in the direction we want. The oroboros (serpent eating its tail) and the lemniscate (infinity symbol) both represent the cyclical, neverending flow of universal energy we all possess. We always have this energy at our disposal to realize our dreams. Are you realizing your full potential? Do you possess latent talents you aren't utilizing? Are you taking appropriate action to reach your goal? Are you connecting with the energies around you to help work toward those goals?

When reversed, the Magician can show us that we are using our powers to manifest our goals to harm others along the way. Are we stepping on other people to reach our goals? Is our end goal harmful to others or ourselves? He can also show us that our goals are not matching up with what we really need at our cores. Are we moving toward what we want or what we need? Are we only taking superficial action to reach a goal that requires deep internal work? The Magician reversed could also be signaling that perhaps we aren't giving ourselves enough credit. Do we see ourselves as powerless victims? Do we think we can't do anything to change the current situation? The Magician is all about our own innate abilities. We have inner power even if we don't believe we do.

II · THE HIGH PRIESTESS

The High Priestess is the feminine balance to the Magician. She
represents our subconscious mind. Like the Magician, she is
a master of her elements. She represents the serenity and all-
knowing wisdom of our intuition. The cross on her chest represents balance. Her predominant color is blue because she is calm

and tranquil. The High Priestess is our own personal connection to the divine. She doesn't have to prove or explain her presence, she just *is*. She holds all the secrets and knowledge on her hidden scroll, and she only reveals them as needed. The light of the moon surrounds her. The moon represents intuitive, illuminating, and undiscovered energies. Are you truly listening to your intuition? Do you have any secrets that you aren't dealing with personally? Are there any secrets you are keeping from others? Why do you feel the need to hold onto these secrets? Are you really connecting with the universal energies around you? Do you take the time to nurture and care for yourself?

When reversed, the High Priestess usually suggests that we have either lost that connection to our intuition or we are simply ignoring it. Your intuition is that calm inner voice you *know* is telling you the truth, even if you don't want to listen. Is your intuitive voice being drowned out by louder ego-driven voices? Are you listening to what those ego-driven voices want and ignoring what your intuition is telling you that you need? Perhaps recent changes have caused a disconnect from that divine inner connection; how can you work to regain it? The High Priestess is all about turning inward and looking deep into your subconscious and working to restore any lost balance. Spending some time in meditation is a good way to reconnect with that inner connection and to better understand yourself at a very basic level.

III · THE EMPRESS

The Empress represents the divine mother. She is a very feminine card and therefore calls on us to embrace our feminine side. She is kind, nurturing, motherly, fertile, sensual, and beautiful. Are you nurturing yourself enough? She could represent our mother or a mother figure in our lives. How is your relationship with this person? The Empress is engulfed in bright yellows and golds that represent the vitality, creativity, and positive energy she emits. Her shield represents the protection we get when we surround ourselves with comforting love. Flourishing wheat surrounds her, a symbol of her nurturing energy. As a symbol of Mother Nature, the green of her cloak represents nature and prosperity. Could connecting more with nature help you achieve your goal? Her cloak is covered in pomegranates, a symbol of fertility. The Empress can also be a symbol of pregnancy. That could mean a literal pregnancy or it could refer to something being "pregnant" with possibilities or an abundance of opportunity. When this card appears, she tells us that our environment and the energies around us are ripe to begin the creation process.

When reversed, the Empress often tells us that we are mothering too much. Are you babying a loved one? Are you being overly protective? This card also sometimes shows us that we aren't giving ourselves the love and care we deserve. Are you putting so much energy into caring for a loved one that you aren't taking care of yourself? Perhaps you are in a codependent relationship with someone. How could you change the situation to form a better more healthy relationship with that person? Nurturing and caring for a child or loved one is a very important thing, but like with all good things they can be taken to an unhealthy extreme. The Empress reminds us to always keep that healthy balance.

IV · THE EMPEROR

The Emperor is the masculine balance to the feminine Empress. He is the deck's father figure. He represents wisdom, leadership, and stability. He is practical and grounding. A lifetime of experience has made him a very wise man. The warm yellow that surrounds the Emperor represents the clarity his advice brings. His deep red robes represent action and power. His long beard and aged face represent the experience he has earned over a lifetime of living. The Egyptian ankh staff he holds represents the stability and balance needed in life. The ram embroidered on his robe speaks to us of action and leadership. The Emperor urges us to add that stability to our lives. He asks us to really see the current situation rationally with our logical brain, and take any necessary action. This card could also represent your father or a father figure in your life. How could this person's advice help you achieve your goal? Perhaps the card represents a new opportunity to take a leadership role in your own life/career or a fatherly role in someone else's.

When reversed, the Emperor usually speaks to us of taking a leadership role or place of power to the extreme. Are you abusing your power? Are you taking advantage of the people around you to move up? Like with everything you can take a positive control too far. Are you too rigid? Could you benefit from being a little more flexible? The Emperor reversed could also be telling you that you lack self-control and aspirations. Could you benefit from a bit more structure? Perhaps setting limits on your own behavior could better help you achieve your goal. Adding some stability and structure could help you reach your goals and get you out of your current situation.

V · THE HIEROPHANT

The Hierophant is all about our traditions and beliefs. He represents a man who holds true to his religious convictions. His red robes speak to us of his passions and structure. The Hierophant's staff, a three-tiered cross, is another nod to his religious beliefs. This symbol is a representation of the Father, the Son, and the Holy Spirit. He is a wealth of religious knowledge and leads his followers well. The keys behind him represent his ability to unlock the doors between our world and the divine. The Hierophant asks us to evaluate our spiritual belief systems. He represents the need to have a strong set of spiritual beliefs whatever those beliefs may be. Are you a religious person? Is your religion or belief system serving you well? Is it time to reevaluate your system of beliefs? Are you really learning the lessons that life is trying to teach you? Besides religious institutions the Hierophant can also represent any group or structured organization. He speaks of conforming to that organization's standards. He could be trying to tell us that we could benefit from more rules and rigid structure.

When reversed, the Hierophant often tells us that we are trying to get away from rigid structure. Perhaps our religion or belief system is no longer benefiting us. Could reexamining some of those beliefs help you move forward? Perhaps the overall rigidity of our lives is becoming a hindrance. Could the structure of your career or an organization be wearing on you? Could you benefit with a little more flexibility in some aspects of your life? What can you change to better help yourself toward your goals? Along with structure the reversed Hierophant speaks to us of breaking away from conformity and societal norms. Are you feeling a lot of societal pressure to be a certain way? Are you doing things because you think you *should* instead of because you actually want to do those things? Don't feel pressured to be someone you aren't.

VI · THE LOVERS

The Lovers is all about love, relationships (romantic or friendships), and everything they encompass. They tell us to follow our hearts and to act with love. With a tender and soft touch, the Lovers gaze longingly into each other's eyes, showing the deep connection and love they feel for one another. The nudity conveys the complete openness and vulnerability needed in our relationships. The blue of the sky represents the openness, emotional awareness, and sensitivity needed to have a healthy relationship. The white lily is a symbol of purity and innocence. The green represents the health and fertility needed to grow your relationships. Green is also the color of your heart chakra. The angel is Raphael, a symbol of communication, key for all of your relationships. This card is also about overall choices in life and realizing the consequences for those choices. If a choice is to be made, don't completely ignore logic; listen to what your heart wants. Our inner voices will help guide us. With this card it is also important to ask yourself: in your relationships are you being honest with yourself and others? Do you feel like you can trust your loved ones? Have you put up barriers to keep people away?

When reversed, the Lovers can be trying to tell us that there is an imbalance in our relationships. Are you treating your loved one the way you would like to be treated? Do you allow yourself to be vulnerable? Are you keeping the lines of communication open? Are you getting the same in return? It is important recognize any imbalance so you can work to rectify it. A reversed Lovers card could also be indicating that we aren't taking full responsibility for past choices we may have made. If you regret any past decisions, what new choices can you make to better your current situation?

VII · THE CHARIOT

When you think about what it would be like to drive a chariot, what do you imagine? Controlling two large horses takes nothing short of sheer will and determination, and that is exactly what this card represents. The Chariot represents moving ourselves forward toward our goal using determination, self-confidence, and control. The blues and subtle violets represent how he inspires those around him with his problem solving skills and persistence. The Chariot is a role model for getting things done. His dual horses, dark and light, represent the balance of positive and negative that makes up the universe. The yellow sun shining behind him represents the vitality and clarity he has regarding his goals. He sees them clearly and will let nothing stop him from getting where he needs to be. If we are struggling, the Chariot tells us that it's time to hunker down and work to get ourselves out of the rut. It is the time to really focus on what you need to do and to do it. What are the things that motivate you? What inspires you? Are you lacking confidence in certain areas? Are there other areas that better deserve your focus?

When reversed, the Chariot often tells us that we are lacking control in certain areas. Perhaps we are letting people walk all over us and aren't asserting ourselves enough. Are there areas in your life in which you need to be more confident and vocal? How can you better move toward your goal? The reversed Chariot can also be trying to tell us that we are taking our need for control to a negative extreme. Are there areas in your life that could benefit from letting go? Perhaps we need to trust more in those around us. Are you harnessing your passions into aggression? Could you better channel that energy into something more positive that could help move you toward your goals? Balance is the goal we should strive for.

VIII · STRENGTH

The Strength card is all about finding that inner courage we were born with to tame the wild beast. She doesn't speak to us of physical strength but of deep-rooted emotional inner strength. The green represents nature and growth, because we all naturally possess this strength and with it we grow as individuals.

The yellow radiates positivity and vitality because this strength is only truly harnessed with positive thinking. The white of her gown represents hope and urges us to never give up, even in the darkest times. The orange represents the comforting and healing energy she emanates. It is not through aggressive means that the beast is tamed; only through love and understanding can we calm it. The lion often represents our inner beast. Those ego driven voices that gnaw at us and aim to drive us mad. Strength urges you not to try and physically *fight* the beast, but rather to try and understand it. When we fight the beast, we give it more power. Treat it with love and compassion, and try to figure out exactly *why* the beast acts the way it does. What is your biggest inner struggle? How can you better work to understand it? What are your inner strengths? Are there any ways you could put a positive spin on whatever's bringing you down?

When reversed, the Strength card could be hinting that our inner strength and confidence are really lacking right now. What can you do to build those back up? Are there things/people in your life that tear you down? How can you eliminate them? Do you doubt yourself? Are you constantly seeking validation from others? You don't need anyone else's approval. Strength urges us to look inside ourselves with a kind and gentle eye and see that we are more than enough just the way we are.

IX · THE HERMIT

The Hermit is a card all about introspection. In today's fast-paced world we often get spun in circles searching outwardly for guidance. Sometimes what we need to do is stop and look inward. He speaks to us of slowing down and taking time to look deep within ourselves for the answers we seek. The deep blues around him symbolize the need to calm and slow down. The colors also remind us of the need to be completely open and vulnerable to ourselves. The Hermit's cloak represents the need to hibernate or isolate ourselves from the busy energy around us. The mountains represent the wisdom and growth he experiences from focusing inward. The six-pointed star is made up of two triangles, one upside-down and one upright. These triangles represent conflicting energies and the star is the balance between them. The yellow radiating from the star represents the clarity we have once we find the answers within ourselves. When you come across the Hermit in a reading, ask yourself: Do I take time to really listen to what my gut is telling me? Do I take time to slow down and just *be*? Could I benefit from meditation? Is my current path still the right one? After some deep introspection we may feel like our original goals are no longer important. It's good to occasionally stop and reevaluate our paths, as it is easy to get caught up in the process and lose sight of our goals.

The reversed Hermit could be trying to tell us that perhaps we are taking solitude to a harmful extreme. Are you isolating yourself, away from things or people you love? Are you so deep in introspection that you are beginning to obsess? Could you benefit from taking a break from your inner search? The reversed Hermit could also be warning of an unwanted isolation, perhaps in a relationship. Do you have a fear of being alone? Are you only staying in a current situation due to fear of isolation? Do you keep busy as a distraction?

X · Wheel of Fortune

The Wheel of Fortune is a card of cycles and change. Change is unavoidable. The events happening right now will not last forever. The Wheel of Fortune speaks to us of karma and destiny and more specifically those changes that seemingly come out of nowhere. These changes in life are neither good nor bad, they just are. I chose purples and oranges, as they are each comprised of two separate colors. Purple is blue and red, while orange is yellow and red. They represent the balance and neutrality of the universe. It is all in how we interpret the changes, and even our interpretations of the changes may change over time. What may seem like a negative change now may change into positive in the long run. Could outside forces be influencing your situation? How do you handle change? Overall the Wheel of Fortune is a positive card about having faith that the universe is looking out for us. While we can't control every aspect of life, we can control how we react to it. The upright Wheel of Fortune usually represents an upcoming positive change, but if you pay close attention to the person falling off the wheel on the right of the card, you'll see that it's also about consequences. This is also a card of karma and reaping what you sow. Do you fully understand the possible consequences to your actions?

When reversed, this card suggests that we are due for a less than favorable change. Could poor decisions have contributed to this change? Karma is still at play even when reversed. Is there anything you can do to rectify those actions? The Wheel of Fortune also urges us to take action and not simply wait for change to come. The reversed wheel can likewise signify that we are resisting change. Why do you resist change? How can you change the way you perceive it?

XI · JUSTICE

It is no wonder that Justice follows the Wheel of Fortune; this card is about dealing with the consequences of our actions. The Justice card is about justice, balance, and responsibility. She reminds us that universal energy is fair and balanced. Justice is a completely pure and neutral card, as is shown by her pure white gown. Her fiery red hair signifies her power, but the calm blues show us that she is not malicious. Justice simply lays out the facts as they are and does not seek to criticize. Her swords symbolize our need to cut through our emotions and to really look at our situation rationally with a logical mind. Could stepping outside of your emotional side help you find clarity? As an outcome card Justice reminds us that the events will unfold exactly as they are supposed to. Do you always logically think through the possible consequences before you act? Could the consequences of previous actions be affecting you now? The scales of Justice represent the necessary balance needed in our lives. Do you feel like your life is in balance? Is there anything you could change to bring balance back into your life?

When reversed, the Justice card usually signifies that we aren't being completely genuine with ourselves. Do you take responsibility for your actions? Do you blame your situation on outside forces? Are there responsibilities you are avoiding? Avoidance keeps us stuck, and checking even small things off of our lists can help us move forward toward our ultimate goal. Justice reversed can also mean that an unfair outcome is on the horizon. Could it be because of previous actions? Now would be a good time to reevaluate your situation and look for any possible changes that could be made to alter that outcome.

XII · The Hanged Man

Unlike the feelings its title conveys, the Hanged Man is not a dark card. As we can see by the look on his face, the Hanged Man is not uncomfortable or struggling. This is a card of suspension, letting go, and productive sacrifice. The light blue background symbolizes this card's serenity. The Hanged Man urges us to suspend our actions and just *be*. Are you taking time to relax? Could your situation benefit from taking a little break? Sometimes we do our best work after we step away from a project for a bit. The Hanged Man also speaks to us of sacrificing and letting go—positive sacrifices for a greater good. The Hanged Man's crossed legs symbolize that we are at a crossroads and need to reevaluate our situation. Now is the time to analyze our situation to look for any areas that are no longer serving us. This is about letting those things go so we can move forward. Are there any thoughts or beliefs that are no longer serving you? Could you benefit from sloughing off all the unnecessary extras? The Hanged Man's halo symbolizes his connection with a higher energy even though he is still deeply grounded by the sturdy tree to which he is bound. The greens and browns represent his connection with the natural energies around him. He uses those energies to help him let go. Could reconnecting with nature help you let go in your current situation?

When reversed, the Hanged Man can signify that we are sacrificing too much. Are you spreading yourself too thin? Are you taking time to take care of yourself? Are you sacrificing everything and getting nothing in return? The reversed Hanged Man can also hint that perhaps we are unwilling to make the necessary sacrifices. Sometimes we hang on to what we know and are comfortable with, even if it is really holding us back. Could you benefit from making some changes?

XIII · DEATH

The Death card is not necessarily about mortality. This card *is* about endings, but more specifically about transitions. Where one situation ends, another begins. Energy is neither created nor destroyed; it simply transitions from one state to another, and this is the basis for this card. Death reminds us that change is inevitable, and it's best to go with that flow of energy and not try and fight it. Transformation can be uncomfortable, but it's when we resist change that we feel pain and struggle. Are you resisting change? How do you react to it? Are there things you could do to better prepare yourself? The bright yellow rising sun in the background represents the new beginning that follows every ending. The white rose signifies purity and hope and that the beauty of the rose is worth a few thorns. Death can represent an abrupt ending or change to an aspect of your life. The rising sun and rose remind us that with all endings are new, wonderful beginnings. There is always hope and light at the end of the tunnel. The Death card continues what the Hanged Man teaches us, showing us that after we let go of whatever is no longer serving us we are left with a fresh new beginning to work toward our goals.

When the Death card comes up reversed, it represents that we are due for a transformation but we are resisting it. What are you afraid of changing? Are there thought processes that can be changed to help ease your fears? It could also be that we are holding on too tightly to the negatives of our transformation. Are you focusing too much on what you have lost and not what's ahead of you? Grieving even the tiniest of changes is completely healthy but it is also important to remember the balance of life. There is always positive amongst the negative; we just have to open our eyes to it.

XIV · TEMPERANCE

Temperance is a card of balance. More specifically, it is a card of keeping balance as we incorporate new things into our lives. As we can see by the red cloth draping around her, she is powerful but more of a powerful calm. Surrounded by blue sky and flowing blue water, she is a tranquil flowing energy that reminds us of the importance of going with the natural flow of things. Do you go with the flow or do you resist change? She continues the Death card's message of not resisting change and going forward in our new beginnings. As she slowly blends the contents of the two vessels, Temperance urges us to mix the new changing aspects of our lives slowly and carefully with the already established aspects. She reminds us not to disrupt the balance as we add new things. Are two significant things in your life merging? Are you taking time to slowly blend them so as to not disrupt the balance? Changing a little bit at a time and then reevaluating is key to maintain that balance. She hints that we have clear vision and are doing a good job of keeping our lives in balance. The yellow and green of this card also pertain to having good balance in the health aspect of our lives.

When Temperance comes up reversed, it is usually trying to tell us that we aren't moving forward in balance. Are there aspects of your life that are taking over other equally important things? Are you moving too quickly into change paying no mind to how the old and new are changing? Temperance reversed can also indicate that we aren't taking care of ourselves health-wise. Are you worried about your health? Are there steps you could take to put yourself on a healthier path?

XV · THE DEVIL

The Devil is a card about the ego-driven voices within us. He represents those negative inner voices that distort our thoughts into beliefs that we are trapped in our situation due to outside forces. The Devil embodies our fears, addictions, harmful instincts, and impulses. Surrounded by red, he is a very strong and powerful card. The deep, dark blue—almost black—shows that he is extremely skilled at creating illusion to make us feel weak and imprisoned. The people he has chained to him aren't struggling because they have chosen to give themselves over to him completely. They are choosing to believe his lies and illusions even though they could remove the chains at any time. Where are you feeling stuck or helpless? How can you stop giving power to the negative forces that try to hold you back? Do you feel unworthy of peace, happiness, and love? Why? Are you indulging in addictive or otherwise harmful behaviors? Are you obsessing over a new project or idea? How can you pull yourself up, away from those lower negative levels of thinking? Remembering that these thoughts and feelings are simply illusions; we can help ourselves move past them and break free of the Devil's control. The Devil is also about getting caught up in indulgences and materialism. Money and objects truly can't buy happiness, and getting too swept up will only bring stress and negativity in the long run.

When reversed, the Devil signifies that we are ready for or already in the process of breaking away from those negative ways of thinking that hold us back. Humans are creatures of habit, and we stick with what we know even if what we know is harmful. The fear of the unknown seems scarier than the negatives we already know. Knowing that our fears are unfounded and not listening to those ego-driven voices are key.

XVI · THE TOWER

The Tower usually represents a sudden and life-altering change. It is usually just as we are getting used to and comfortable in our situations that life decides to throw us for a loop. The Tower is a card of change, destruction, vulnerability, exposure, and breaking down walls. The blues and violets that fill this card represent that comfort and security. The lightning, however, and red fire suddenly destroy that comfort and security. The Tower could hint at a break-up, death, sudden loss, or any significant change. Even though The Tower often brings painful and uncomfortable change, it also speaks of the importance of working through that pain. It is important that we feel those emotions and actually work through the situation so we can grow and come out the other side a stronger more balanced person. Do you remember to take care of yourself during tough times? Are there any lessons you can take away from this situation? The Tower could signify a change due to outside forces or it could mean that we have built up a life or situation that is doing more harm than good and needs to be torn down. Are you being honest with yourself and others? Have you built up walls of protection to keep others at arm's length? When we build walls to keep out the negative, we also keep out the positive. Now is the time to let ourselves be vulnerable so we can experience all the energy the universe has to offer.

When reversed, the Tower usually signifies that we are resisting a significant change. What is holding you back? If fear of the pain and discomfort is keeping you stuck, it's important to remember that it will be worth it in the long run. We are strong enough to handle any uncomfortable situations, and it is working through the negatives that truly allow us to enjoy and appreciate the positives in life.

XVII · THE STAR

The Star is a very spiritual card and is full of hope and rejuvenation. After the chaos of the Tower, the Star brings with it
a fresh new start full of hope, peace, cleansing, and healing.
Have you ever wished upon a star? Stars have long since been
a symbol of guidance, hope, and positive things to come, and

that perfectly sums up this card. The deep, rich blues speak to us of her calming and comforting nature. She is nude because she is pure and innocent in her fresh start. The healing yellow of the stars shines down on her. The Star really represents the light at the end of the Tower's destructive tunnel, speaking to us of how much we grow and transform after we work through turmoil. The Star shows us that we are moving into a very positive and loving phase of our lives. Her two vessels flow endlessly, supplying healing and rejuvenating waters. As a very spiritual card she also symbolizes a renewed connection with our higher powers and a deeper, stronger bond to our faith. Do you follow the guidance of your higher power? Do you allow yourself time to relax? Do you truly nurture yourself and others?

When the Star card appears reversed, it usually signifies that we aren't feeling the hope and rejuvenation we had anticipated. Instead we are feeling negativity and despair. When reversed she can also speak to us about a loss of faith. Are you stuck in negative rumination? Do you have faith in yourself? After the trauma from the Tower, we may feel weak and broken. Do you see yourself as a victim? What do you need to regain confidence in yourself? How can you pay less attention to those ego-driven voices that tear you down? Taking some time for self-care and giving yourself a break physically and mentally can really help bring you back to where you belong.

XVIII · The Moon

The Moon represents all those repressed thoughts, feelings, insecurities, and fears we hold down deep inside us. The Moon tarot card is almost entirely blue to show us how emotionally charged it is. She is a card of illusion. Is every aspect of your situation really as it appears to be? The Moon speaks to us of our ability to project our subconscious fears and anxieties into the world around us and the way our minds can play tricks on us. It is just human nature. The dog and wolf symbolize the internal battle between reality and our biggest fears and sources of struggle. The Moon wants to remind us of our tendency to project or fear the worst so we don't let ourselves become slaves to negativity. Are you feeling blocked or trapped because of your fears and insecurities? Are you allowing your fears to distract you from the reality around you? Perhaps you would benefit from some deep internal work or meditation to discover what is holding you back at a subconscious level and how you can best face those fears and insecurities. The lobster and crustaceans in general have tough outer shells, representative here of our propensity to build up walls to keep all those insecurities and emotions locked away. The Moon card urges us to break down those walls and work through and feel the emotions. Now is the time to get grounded and to use our intuition to diffuse the cloud of illusion and get back on track.

When the Moon comes up reversed, it usually means that we are struggling to work through those subconscious blocks or that we are feeling trapped in the illusion. What is causing you to hesitate or feel stuck? Are your thoughts based in reality? Could you benefit from changing your perspective? The reversed Moon can also signify that we are in a very psychic/intuitive place but are very confused or not open to any messages. Write the messages down; they may become clearer in the future.

XIX · THE SUN

The Sun is the bright light after the subtle, dark Moon. This is a very positive card, representing the hope we can always count on—even if the sky is cloudy, the sun always rises without fail. He instills a sense of energetic confidence, light, and illumination. The Sun illuminates the darkness and shadows while also removing the confusion and doubt. After the deep internal work of the Moon, the Sun shows us that we are reaping the rewards. He tells us that success and positive energy is right around the corner. The sunflowers represent the need to always strive for a stronger connection with our higher spiritual power just as sunflowers follow the sun across the sky. The Sun is also a very energetic card. Its bright yellows and oranges speak of his bright vital energy. Are you feeling in a very good place physically and mentally? Are you starting any new projects? Now is a good time to do just that. You have a lot of enthusiastic positive energy in your corner. The Sun is the ultimate "yes" card, reassuring you that all your hard work is about to pay off and you are indeed on the right path.

When reversed, the Sun can signify that we are taking our positivity to a negative extreme. Are you being realistic with your goals? Are you overly confident? Could you benefit from reevaluating and grounding yourself and your goals? The Sun reversed can also mean we are having a hard time finding the positives in our situation. You may be in a depressive state. Are there any blockages that are holding you back? Is there any aspect of your situation in which you could use some clarity? Even when reversed, the Sun is rarely negative; remember that any blocks or setbacks are only going to be short-lived.

XX · JUDGEMENT

Judgement can often seem like a very scary word. This card, however, is not negative at all. Judgement speaks to us of transitions, rebirth, and decisions. The gentle blues of this card represent peaceful and tranquil transitions. A stage or situation in our lives might be coming to an end. We can benefit from looking back at our journey. What have you learned? Would you change anything? Judgement often urges for an overall self-evaluation, because we can only truly move forward after we have learned the lessons life is trying to teach us. Judgement also often conveys putting any misdeeds and negative energy from our pasts behind us. It is a card of moving forward and atoning for any sins, allowing for a new fresh start or a blank slate. The angel Gabriel blowing his horn also speaks to us of a higher calling. After learning what one situation has to teach us we can move on to aspire bigger and greater things. Judgement is also a card of decisions. We cannot leave everything to chance, and not making a decision is still a decision. We must often make difficult choices, but we can never go wrong by following logic and listening to our intuition.

When reversed, Judgement can indicate that we are being too hard on ourselves. Do you doubt your ability to make good decisions? How can you rebuild that confidence in yourself? Do you judge yourself or others too harshly? Judgement reversed could also hint that we aren't truly learning the lessons the universe is trying to teach us. This could cause a feeling of being stuck or blocked from moving forward. What lessons could you learn from your current or past situations? Are you connecting with your higher power for guidance?

XXI · THE WORLD

The last of the major arcana and the end of the Fool's journey,
the World represents completion, wholeness, success, endings,
and new beginnings. A situation or life stage may be coming to
an end and with it comes a sense of completion and closure.
The bright colors signify that this is not a sad card. The World

is about seeing all of your hard work pay off and enjoying the rewards. It speaks to us of fulfillment and joy. This is about happy endings transforming into new opportunities and fresh starts. We can then start the cycle all over again with the next situation or life stage. The wreath has long since been a symbol of victory. Adorned here with a ribbon wrapped in an infinity symbol further emphasizes the universe's cyclical nature. Each corner is adorned with a figure representing one of the four fixed signs of the zodiac: Leo, Taurus, Scorpio, and Aquarius. These figures further symbolize our success and completion by implying the stars have aligned in our favor. Now is the time to celebrate our accomplishments and reward ourselves for all the hard work it took to get here.

When reversed, the World often indicates that we aren't taking the necessary action to reach our ultimate goals. Perhaps we aren't doing the hard dirty work that our situation requires and are trying to take the easy path. Are you trying to cheat the system to get to your goal? Are you lying to yourself or others to move forward? We do ourselves a disservice by trying to avoid the lessons and hard work that builds character and make us stronger. The reversed World can also illustrate that a situation is coming to an end but we are lacking that sense of closure or completion. Could communication with others in the situation help you gain closure? Sometimes time is all we can use to gain clarity and the ability to move forward.

THREE

⌒

MINOR ARCANA

Suit of Wands

The suit of wands is representative of the element Fire. Red is the symbolic color of fire.

This suit is about action, movement, primal energy, and gut reactions. The Wands represent the fire within us, the spark that drives us forward and pushes us to make our dreams and goals reality. They represent taking initiative and action instead of just waiting for things to happen. These cards are about fast actions and burning passions. On the flip side, however, Wands can signify hot tempers, acting impulsively, lack of direction, and aimless wandering.

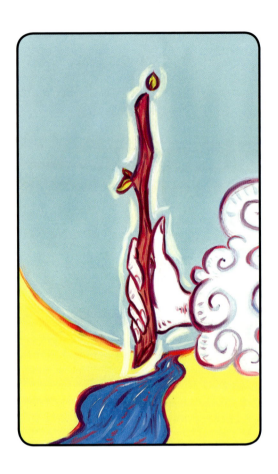

ACE OF WANDS

The Ace of Wands is a giant neon blinking sign telling us "Go create." It represents creativity, inspiration, beginnings, and ideas. This card is about raw, burning passions. The Ace of Wands urges us to harness all of that passion and energy and make all our ideas and dreams reality. Now is the time to act on our ideas instead of simply thinking about our dreams; the card demands we act on them. Like all aces, the Ace of Wands is simply a seed that we must plant within ourselves and nurture its growth. This card shows us all our potential successes, and it is on us to do the work to actually make that success happen. What are your passions? What drives you? In what direction do you want to go with your new plan?

Reversely, the Ace of Wands can signal a lack of drive, inspiration, or passion. It may signal restlessness, or the lack of a clear path. We may feel trapped by our current responsibilities and unable to move forward to new ideas. Taking some times to meditate and reevaluate may help. See where in your life you can let some things go and where you may be able to add a few new projects, little by little.

TWO OF WANDS

The Two of Wands is about deciding on a new idea and beginning to put that plan to action. The figure in this card has decisively chosen the wand he wants and is now embarking to make that idea a reality. This card is about taking an idea and moving it into the planning stages. He holds the world in his hands and a vast array of options and possibilities lay out in front of him. When not referring to a business or project reading the Two of Wands can be, as all twos, indicative of making a choice between two options. This card in particular hints that you have weighed both options completely and are ready to decide. He doesn't seem torn between the two wands; he knows exactly which one he wants and is already moving forward with his choice. What is your plan of action now that you have made a decision? Are you acting from a knowledgeable place or are you acting impulsively?

When reversed, the Two of Wands can indicate a failure to make a decision or a fear of moving forward. This card urges us to weigh all of the possible options and have confidence in our decision being the best possible with the current information. It also serves as a reminder that we will be able to handle any obstacles that appear in the future.

THREE OF WANDS

The Three of Wands is a card of reflection, expansion, and growth. The figure in this card is overseeing all he has built so far. He takes time to reflect on how far he has come and all the ideas he has for the future. The Three of Wands show us that we have put our plans into action and while everything is progressing nicely, we need to keep working and using ideas to ensure that progress continues until the end. This is a card of growing and expanding our business or projects. Though his wands are firmly planted in the ground, he holds on to them just in case they need to be rearranged. The Three of Wands is also a reminder to remain flexible as we progress since we don't know what the future will bring. What plans have you set in motion? How are these plans progressing? Could any of them use any tweaking?

When reversed, the Three of Wands can be a sign that we are struggling to get our business or project off the ground, and are feeling overwhelmed and perhaps like we bit off more than we could chew. Reevaluating our plans and breaking up our tasks into small easier to accomplish tasks can help us get more done without feeling stressed.

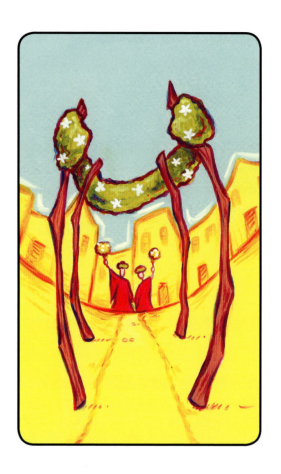

Four of Wands

The Four of Wands is a card of stability, celebration, and marriage. It can be a literal or symbolic marriage. It often represents a coming together of people; perhaps it is a romantic marriage, a business partnership, or simply a coming together of loved ones in celebration. This coming together of people leads to a solidifying of our foundation, bringing with it much more stability. The Four of Wands can indicate an upcoming reason for celebration. It could be a marriage, reaching a new milestone, or finally completing that big project. The Four of Wands is a very positive card and most often speaks of good energy to follow, specifically in our family and home environments. It is also a reminder to keep going because all of our hard work is going to pay off immensely. Are you taking the time to enjoy your family and home life? What are your plans for the future after the celebration ends?

When reversed, the Four of Wands can indicate tension or unstable ground at home or with our family. Perhaps there are ongoing transitions in our homes that are causing tensions. It can also signal a feeling of isolation and disconnect from friends and loved ones. The Four of Wands is a reminder of the importance of having supportive and loving people around us.

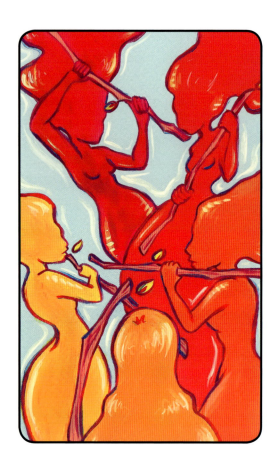

Five of Wands

The Five of Wands is a card of conflict and challenges. This card often acts as a warning of upcoming conflict, specifically with others around us. The fighting and competition with those around us is holding us back from our goals. However, not all conflict is negative; this card could indicate a healthy competition among our peers. The Five of Wands serves as a reminder to not let ourselves get caught up in the anger and frustration of competition and to remain respectful to ourselves and our competitors. This card can also indicate personal inner struggles. Perhaps we are fighting with many different options and don't know which one to choose. This card reminds us to step back and weigh all the options together fairly to see which is best. Can you find common ground with the other party? Why do you feel the need to fight? Could your issue be solved with better means of communication? Could you benefit from a mediator?

When reversed, the Five of Wands often represents avoiding conflict or competition simply out of the fear of losing. Some competition is necessary in life, and without trying we will never know if we could. Failure is simply checking one option off of our lists; there are still many other things to try. The Five of Wands reversed can also be an indication that our conflicts are coming to an end.

Six of Wands

The Six of Wands is a card of victory, success, and receiving recognition for our accomplishments. This card depicts a celebratory parade for the victor. As he carries his laurel wreath, the crowd around him raises their wands and rejoices together in his success. His white horse signifies that his victory was well deserved and earned by hard work and determination. He was not just handed this success. The Six of Wands is a confidence builder that suggests our hard work is about to be recognized. It urges us to have faith in ourselves and our abilities to make our goals happen, and to build and keep a strong confidence in ourselves. Can you accept success humbly? Now that you have reached success, what do you do next? Did anyone else help you reach your goal?

When reversed, the Six of Wands can indicate a lack of self-esteem and confidence. It urges us to seek support from others or perhaps build our confidence despite what others think about our progress. When reversed it can also indicate that we aren't getting the recognition that we wanted, which may be in the form of negative feedback. Using feedback to grow, even if it isn't what we want to hear, can help us grow into where we want to be in the future.

SEVEN OF WANDS

The Seven of Wands represents taking a stand, competition, and determination. The figure in this card has worked hard to get on higher ground and he's not letting anything knock him back down. The Seven of Wands urges us to take a stand and face our challenges and competition head on, which means facing not only our outward challenges but our inner demons as well. We often need to take a stand within ourselves. This card can also serve as a reminder that as we succeed in our ventures and climb up the ladder, we will face new and different challenges. The Seven of Wands reminds us to not get discouraged with those challenges and just keep going. What benefits can you gain from your position? Are you being defensive?

When reversed, the Seven of Wands often illustrates being overwhelmed with our responsibilities in life. It urges us to rebuild our confidence by delegating responsibilities where possible and setting small more attainable goals. This card reversed can also indicate that we are trying so hard to avoid conflict that we aren't able to move toward our goals. Not everyone is going to like us or agree with us. Accepting that we can't please everyone and realizing that conflict is sometimes a necessary part of life can help us get back on track.

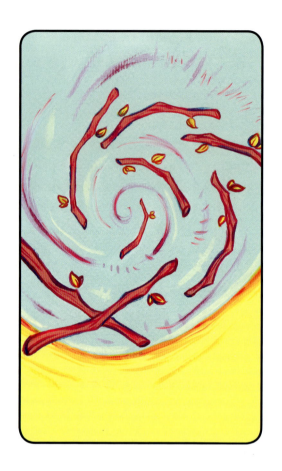

EIGHT OF WANDS

This card is all about movement and travel. The eight wands represent ideas and inspiration. With forward momentum, the wands push you toward your end goals. Are you starting a new project or do you have a project you've wanted to start? The eight wands are flowing to a center point, indicating a very focused energy. We don't let any distractions take away focus, and it is with sheer determination that we are working toward our goal. If you aren't already, this card might be telling you that you need to really focus and get your hands dirty to get what you are seeking. Do you go with the flow? Could your goal benefit from a change in focus?

Reversely, the Eight of Wands reminds us that with everything comes balance. Are you starting a new project without fully comprehending what you are getting into? If we are charging full steam ahead a reversed Eight of Wands might be telling us to slow down and rethink our plan. This card may also be forewarning of some delays or that we are in unstable times. Sometimes it's best to slow down a bit until we are in a better place or mindset to push forward.

NINE OF WANDS

The Nine of Wands is a card of resilience, perseverance, and not giving up. The man is beaten and tired. The wall of wands represents all of his current obstacles and struggles, but despite all that, he isn't letting himself crumble. The Nine of Wands shows us coming to the end of a situation, but we have come to that one last obstacle we need to get past to finally finish. This card urges us to not feel defeated in the face of adversity but rather to face it head on and push through. The Nine of Wands can also urge us to be cautious on the road ahead to avoid any unnecessary risks. We may encounter a lot of obstacles on our current path, but this card reminds us that in the end it will be worth it. Are you prepared to see your goals through to completion? Do you need help? What previous lessons learned could help you now? Do you stand your ground?

When reversed, the Nine of Wands can represent a time of feeling trapped or under constant attack in our current responsibilities. It may indicate a feeling that everyone is always out to get us. Playing the role of the victim keeps us stuck. The Nine of Wands reversed urges us to take the action necessary to break out of that mindset and get ourselves back on a healthy path forward.

TEN OF WANDS

The Ten of Wands is a card of hard work, responsibility, success, and completion. This card is finally bringing in that last bundle of wood. When we put our ideas into actions it can be tiring, stressful, and often burdensome work, but it is all worth it in the end. We are exhausted, but we are finished and have succeeded at our goal. The Ten of Wands is a sign that all of our hard work is about to pay off or is already paying off. It can also indicate that our upcoming projects are going to take a lot of hard work and skill to be seen to completion, but as long as we keep at it we will reach our goals. The Ten of Wands can also act as reminder to not take on too much at one time and risk becoming overworked. We need to know when to say no to others. Are you prepared for success?

When reversed, the Ten of Wands usually signals that we are taking on too much and that it is starting to affect our quality of work. It shows the feeling of being weighed down and stuck under piles of to-do lists. This could be physical work or represent anxieties and worries we take on. The Ten of Wands reversed urges us to reevaluate our responsibilities and anxieties and delegate where we can, and let go of the things that we have no control over. Are you feeling overworked? Is it time to break things down and regroup? Could your productivity benefit from a break?

Page of Wands

The Page of Wands is about that spark of a new idea or those "light bulb" moments. This card represents new beginnings, enthusiastic energy, and sudden creativity. He encourages us to use that energy to create all of those new ideas and projects we have in our heads. Just like all pages, however, the Page of Wands can be very impulsive and acts before he thinks, which can lead to a lot of trouble. He is very enthusiastic and full of energy but can also have a naive quality to him that's almost annoying with his constant pestering. Like all the pages, he can represent a messenger. He often brings word of unexpected news, a welcomed surprise, or brand new information. Does this represent an aspect of yourself or someone else in your life?

Reversely, the Page of Wands can be immature and childish, lacking any drive or ambition. He can symbolize getting stuck in the mundane of everyday life. This card reminds us of the importance of relighting that spark within ourselves. Finding that muse or environment that always gets the creative juices flowing can help us feel unstuck and get us back on track to our goals.

KNIGHT OF WANDS

The Knight of Wands takes the new idea we got with the Page of Wands and puts it into action. This Knight is passionate and driven like the Queen of Wands, and he is charismatic and charming like the King of Wands. However, being a knight, he has yet to truly perfect those skills. While he is full of energy and drive, he can be impatient and impulsive and has a tendency to rush into things. He's an "act now, think later" type who often fearlessly jumps in before thinking about all the consequences. The Knight of Wands is a reminder to hold onto our passionate energy in our projects and also balance it with some occasional moments of rechecking that we are still on the right path.

When reversed, the Knight of Wands can indicate a frustration with obstacles and feeling stuck in our progress. It can symbolize a feeling of having no control leading to grasping at straws. The Knight of Wands reversed is a reminder to slow down occasionally to reevaluate our current situations. It's too easy to get swept up in the "go, go, go"; now may be the perfect time to slow down and think before we act.

QUEEN OF WANDS

The Queen of Wands is a ruler of passion and truly personifies that *fire* in all of us that drives us to do and create. She pushes us to harness her fiery energy and use it to transform the world around us. The Queen of Wands pushes us to do and to act. This is not a "sit back and wait" card. She is warm and confident. Nothing stands in her way when it comes to achieving her goals. She reminds us to be confident and independent. She urges us to be bold, strong, and courageous in the face of adversity. The Queen of Wands reminds us that we can do anything we put our minds to. She is unafraid to scorch those who get in her way so be careful to not get burned with this card. Do you recognize her energy in yourself or someone around you? How can these traits help move you forward?

When reversed, the Queen of Wands can indicate a person in our lives who is manipulative and controlling. This person is pushy, arrogant, and doesn't care who they step on to get what they want. Letting go of those characteristics within ourselves or removing people like that from our lives can help us move forward. In a reversed position she can also indicate that we are lacking confidence in our current situation.

King of Wands

The King of Wands is a king of passion. He is a natural leader and very goal oriented. He is able to attract many followers to his cause with his charisma and charm. He represents a very driven and strong-willed individual and can act as a reminder to harness those characteristics within us to reach our current goals. However, the King of Wands can also be somewhat arrogant in his pursuits. He is often compared to that artist who is truly amazing and talented and has an ego to match. This card can be a reminder to keep that ego in check. When not referring to a person, the King of Wands can show us that a new opportunity is right around the corner and we need to jump on it. How can you harness these traits to help in your current situation?

When reversed, the King of Wands can show us that we are setting ourselves up for failure by setting our expectations too high. It can show that we are being egotistical and dramatic in our passions and could benefit from bringing things back down to a realistic level. Setting small attainable goals will help us reach our goal without the added feeling of failure.

Suit of Cups

The Suit of Cups is representative of the element Water. Blue is the symbolic color of water. Cups represent our emotions, creativity, relationships, friendships, and love. This suit speaks more of thinking with our hearts instead of using logic, and bringing up our raw emotional responses to situations. The negative aspect to the suit of cups can reflect repressed emotions or being overly emotional. Reversely, cups can also indicate that that we are following our hearts too much and not thinking logically in a situation.

ACE OF CUPS

The Ace of Cups is like the beginning of a great love, full of promise, overwhelming emotions, and powerful connections. This is a very positive card in general. It indicates that love and following our heart is a very important aspect of our current situation. That may be a romantic love, new relationship, or simply following our hearts in a new business partnership. The Ace of Cups can also be indicative of creative energy, love, and emotions overflowing into our lives. This is a card of compassion and sharing that creative energy and love with those around us. Now is a time to create wonderful things and spread joy. Are you evaluating your situation from a place of love?

When reversed, the Ace of Cups can represent the need to regain an emotional balance in our lives. It can show that we are overflowing with negative emotions and all of that energy is spilling into the rest of our lives. However, it can also be a signal that we are repressing our emotions and not letting ourselves feel and move forward. The Ace of Cups reversed reminds us of emotional balance's importance and not letting ourselves swing to either extreme.

Two of Cups

The Two of Cups represents a perfect, harmonious balance between two people in a relationship. Similar to the Lovers card, the Two of Cups is often considered a soul mate card. It shows the caring, nurturing, mutual respect, and love that come with finding our perfect match. This card is more specifically about the perfect emotional connection between two people who are meant for each other. The Two of Cups can suggest a marriage or upcoming engagement in a romantic relationship, or it can simply indicate finding that kind of balance with a friend. This card could also signify the perfect partnership in business ventures. This is a very positive, emotionally driven card. Occasionally, the Two of Cups can be a reminder to find that nurturing, caring, respectful relationship within our selves. Are you open to new relationships? Do you treat others as you would like to be treated in relationship?

The Two of Cups reversed often indicates a lack of balance in a current relationship or with ourselves. It can represent superficial relationships, perhaps due to lack of trust or putting up walls. When reversed, this card indicates that our relationships or partnerships aren't on level ground.

Three of Cups

The Three of Cups is about people coming together for a common good. It is about friendship, celebration, community, and togetherness. This card illustrates a need to be social and spend some time with friends and loved ones. The Three of Cups is about celebrating and enjoying a break with our closest friends.

It is about support, sisterhood, family, and joy. The Three of Cups is sometimes compared to a bridal shower in that it often symbolizes celebrating the completion of a major milestone in our lives. It is also a reminder to let us take a break and let go even in the most stressful of times. Letting ourselves enjoy life and letting our walls down with loved ones is often the most therapeutic solution in tough times. Are you giving yourself the recognition you deserve? Can you welcome and accept joy and love in your life?

When reversed, the Three of Cups can indicate a feeling of isolation or perhaps a feeling of being trapped in the need to conform to a group or the world around us. In a relationship reading, the Three of Cups reversed could be indicative of a third person coming into a relationship possibly in the form of an affair or love triangle.

Four of Cups

The Four of Cups is a card of meditation, reevaluation, and boredom. It can be a sign that we need to reevaluate and look within ourselves for guidance in our current situation. The woman doesn't let outside distractions break her concentration. Another interpretation of this card is boredom, making the woman uninterested and not amused by the offer of yet another cup. The Four of Cups can indicate we are growing tired of our mundane, unchanging environment and could benefit from changing things up a bit. The perfectly aligned cups can also be a sign that we are becoming obsessed with something in our lives. Are you feeling stuck in the ordinary? Could you benefit from switching up a few things?

When reversed, the Four of Cups can imply that we are looking too deeply into ourselves and missing out on the world around us. The woman is so deep in thought that she doesn't even see the fourth cup. It can also show that we are being too stubborn in our current situation, by purposefully ignoring a solution that is right in front of us. The Four of Cups reversed reminds us to open our eyes to the world around us and not to ignore solutions that we might not like simply because they are different.

Five of Cups

The Five of Cups is a card of focusing on a disappointment while ignoring the hope that is right next to us. The water flowing from the spilled cups indicates that the disappointment is more emotional or mental in nature than it is physical. The Five of Cups can be an indicator that we are wallowing in self-pity.

The man is so preoccupied with his spilt cups that he can't even see the shining new cups right behind him. Those shining new cups represent hope. This card urges us to let go of past disappointments so we can move forward. This is a card of grieving but the message is that we should not not let ourselves focus so much on the loss that we lose sight of our own path. How does negatively dwelling on the loss help you? Does your judgment feel clouded because of this negative focus?

When reversed, the Five of Cups can signal that we are ready to move forward and accept our losses and forgive those who have wronged us. However, it can also indicate that we are ignoring painful past memories and not learning from them. Moving on and working through our problems is healthy, but being in denial about our problems isn't. We need to work through our problems, be able to move on from them.

SIX OF CUPS

The Six of Cups is a card of nostalgia, generosity, remembering our childhoods, and our inner child. This card can indicate a need to tap into our inner child and rediscover that carefree joy we had as children. The Six of Cups can also indicate that we are getting too swept up in the logistics and responsibilities of adulthood; we could benefit from some simple playtime. It can also signify our actual children or children to come. This card may represent a generous and caring nature represented by the mother sharing her flowering cup with her son. The Six of Cups can also indicate the return of a parental figure or aspect of our childhood that we haven't experienced in a while. Are you caring and generous to those around you? Are you getting those in return?

When reversed, the Six of Cups often indicates that we are holding on too strongly to our past in a way that hinders our ability to be in the present and plan for the future. It can also be indicative of bad memories or possible abuse from our childhood that is still affecting us today. Reversed, the Six of Cups can also be a sign for fertility issues or disciplinary problems with our children.

Seven of Cups

The Seven of Cups is a card of getting our heads stuck in the clouds. It is about fantasy, daydreaming, and the reminder that dreams must be eventually put into action to realize them. This card can represent getting swept up in illusions of what "could be" and not focusing on the here and now. It reminds us to differentiate between the imaginary and reality so we don't become stuck in our thoughts. The Seven of Cups can indicate a need to ask ourselves if we are seeing the truth in a current situation or if someone or something is trying to pull wool over our eyes. It is also a reminder to avoid temptation, as not all the cups are filled with positive things—some might come back to bite us. Do you feel bombarded with too many options? How many of the options are realistic? Are you feeling distracted?

When reversed, the Seven of Cups can indicate that we are not using our imagination enough or perhaps we could benefit from following our dreams more. This card can also signify an intense fear of the future. It is a very powerful reminder to not get swept up in the what-ifs of life and to let go of fear and remain in the here and now.

Eight of Cups

The Eight of Cups is a card of transitions and travel. A cloaked figure leaves all that they know behind in hopes of better things to come. This card is about tying up emotional loose ends and moving forward and away from those things that no longer serve us emotionally. The Eight of Cups represents making a choice to move away from things we still might love but we know are no longer serving us or letting us grow spiritually or emotionally. No one is forcing us to go—we just know it is best for us. This could represent leaving a relationship, even when others tell us we are crazy for doing so, or it could be leaving that successful job in order to do what we truly love. The Eight of Cups is about following our hearts even when it sometimes doesn't feel logical. How are you handling any current transitions? Do you feel prepared for the journey?

When reversed, the Eight of Cups may represent feeling stuck in an aspect of our lives that emotionally is draining but logically we don't feel like we can leave. It can remind us of the importance of our emotional and mental health and if our current aspect is not contributing it may be time to move on. The Eight of Cups reversed can also indicate that we feel like we are constantly wondering and don't feel stable. Grounding ourselves may be exactly what we need.

NINE OF CUPS

The Nine of Cups represents overall happiness and contentment in all aspects of our lives. This card is often considered
the "wish card" because it is seen as a sign that we are on the
path to emotional joy and fulfillment, often on a materialistic
level. The Nine of Cups is also a card that reminds us to live

in the moment and count our blessings. Enjoy what you have now, for you may not have it forever. There is also a level of pride to this card, as seen on the somewhat smug look on the man's face. He is very proud of what he has and isn't afraid to show off his treasures on his most predominant shelf. Can you let go of your worries and enjoy right now? How can you make the feeling of contentment last?

When reversed, the Nine of Cups can be seen as a card of not quite getting all that you desire. In tarot, tens are usually seen as overall fulfillment and completion, so the Nine of Cups is sometimes viewed as "that one missing cup." It could be an indication that we are focusing too much on what we don't have and not giving all of our current blessings the attention they deserve. The reversed Nine of Cups can also be an indicator of addiction. Perhaps we have become too enthralled in our desires and they've begun to take over.

Ten of Cups

The Ten of Cups is all about emotional fulfillment. This card is that peak moment of happy ending in a romantic movie just before the credits roll. The happy soulmates embrace as they look over the horizon. The Ten of Cups is the ultimate positive relationship and happy ending card. The ten shining cups represent the beautiful emotional connection these two share. They have worked hard to get where they are and have their entire future together. The Ten of Cups can also represent a very good outcome to the situation if you follow your heart.

When reversed, the Ten of Cups can also represent a cinematic happy ending but only in the sense that movies stop on a high point; they don't show the long haul. Most movie relationships are based on temporary emotions and don't show what it really takes to stand the test of time. This card asks us to be aware of superficial relationships and not see them as more than they are. The reversed Ten of Cups can indicate that we are getting caught up in the image of a perfect family and ignoring issues in the current relationship. This card can also shine light on any neglect in our current relationships or situations.

Page of Cups

The Page of Cups is a messenger of love and inspiration. He is young, fresh, and new. This card could bring news of an upcoming creative project or simply a rush of inspiration. The fish in his cup represents that sudden new inspiration. This is a card of dreams, aspirations, and new relationships. Pages of all suits are messengers; this page specifically can indicate a message from a loved one. It can act as a reminder to listen to our emotions and intuition. If we feel stuck, listening inward may help us move forward.

When reversed, the Page of Cups can represent someone who is emotionally immature or is escaping into a dream world instead of dealing with his or her problems. The reversed Page of Cups can occasionally point to substance abuse in an effort to escape a situation. The Page of Cups in this position could also be someone who is prone to emotional outbursts and reacts to situations very immaturely, such as by throwing temper tantrums. When not representing a person, the Page of Cups reversed could be indicative of a creative or intuitive block.

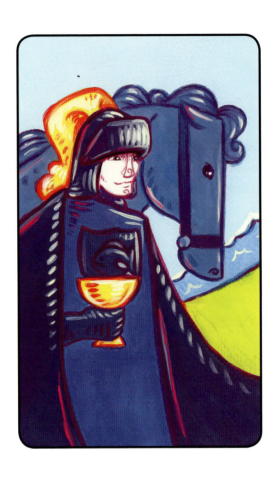

KNIGHT OF CUPS

The Knight of Cups is the type to sweep us off our feet. He is very in touch with his emotions and is ruled by his heart, not his head. He uses his control over his emotions to seduce and romance those around him. The Knight of Cups is extremely attractive to all of those around him. He is completely enthralled with the general idea of love, sometimes even more than the specific person he is trying to romance. While the Knight is very skilled in the art of romance, he has much to learn when it comes to the true meaning of love. The Knight of Cups can also be seen as encouragement to take all that previous inspiration we gained with the Page of Cups and put our creativity to good use. Now is the perfect time to work on making our ideas reality.

The Knight of Cups reversed can warn of an event or person that seems perfect and is extremely seductive at first but later reveals itself to be the complete opposite. This may be a relationship that was perfect but then turns emotionally unstable, or it could be a situation that seemed perfect but later turned out to be a lie. The Knight of Cups reversed urges us to be aware and careful.

QUEEN OF CUPS

The Queen of Cups is the nurturing, kind, and feminine balance to her King of Cups. She is a wonderfully caring wife and mother. The Queen of Cups is very similar to the High Priestess in that she is a very powerful intuition card. She urges you to trust your gut and inner voice. She is also a very empathetic ruler capable of reading the emotions of others, sometimes even before they can. This card urges us to use our compassion and follow our hearts to find a solution to the situation at hand. She shows us that by using our creativity we can move toward accomplishing our goals. How can these traits help you in your current situation? Do you see these traits in yourself or someone around you?

The reversed Queen of Cups is often a sign that we are repressing our emotions or that we are ignoring them completely. It can also signify a need to reconnect with your intuition and inner guides. Like the King of Cups, the Queen reversed can also represent someone who is overly emotional or manipulating people around them to get what they want. This may be a good time to cut someone like that out of our lives.

KING OF CUPS

The King of Cups is a very kind and compassionate ruler. He is a family man and a loving husband and father. This card truly represents the balance between our emotional selves and our intellectual selves. The King of Cups is in full control of his emotions but he does not repress them, rather he uses them to his advantage. He is all about empathy and truly connecting with those around him. The King of Cups urges us to be emotionally mature and balanced in our lives. When not referring to a person this card can simply urge you to find that intellectual and emotional balance. Could you benefit from getting in touch with your emotional side?

When reversed, the King of Cups often refers to a person who is extremely emotionally toxic. This person may be manipulative and emotionally unstable. It can also represent a person who is extremely flirtatious and uses those kind emotions and loving ways to get whatever they want. The King of Cups can indicate someone who has given so much emotional energy to those around them that they are neglecting themselves. It can also simply represent someone who has let their emotions get the better of them.

Suit of Swords

The suit of swords is representative of the element Air. Yellow is the symbolic color of Air. This suit represents our mind, thinking, perception, observation, ideas, communication, and consciousness. The sword is a symbol of power and cutting. When used with care, the sword can be a very powerful and helpful weapon; however, it can also be very destructive and dangerous. Our minds are just like the double-edged sword. We are filled with both positive and negative thoughts. We choose which type receives our power. The negative side of the suit of swords can indicate ego-driven voices, verbal abuse, anger, guilt, and a lack of empathy.

ACE OF SWORDS

The Ace of Swords is the ultimate "thinking" card. It represents pure thought, new ideas, and inspiration. The Ace of Swords can represent the perfect time for new ideas and starting new projects. This card is all about cutting through the distractions and opening our minds. The Ace of Swords urges us to use our logical minds to solve our current situation and not let our emotions cloud our judgment. This card can also indicate a need to let go of those aspects of our life that don't allow us to think clearly. The Ace of Swords urges us to seek truth and to fully become aware of our surroundings in the current situation. Do you feel distracted? How can you simplify your life?

When reversed, the Ace of Swords can indicate a lack of clarity or a misunderstanding of our current situation. Now may be a good time to try and break things down into simpler bits of information so it can be better understood. The Ace of Swords reversed can also indicate a lot of new ideas but not putting them into action; perhaps we have so many ideas that we don't know which one is best. Could making a list of the pros and cons help?

TWO OF SWORDS

The Two of Swords is about indecision and failure to choose. This card can show that when faced with a decision, we'd rather put our head in the sand and refuse to even deal with them. Making a decision can be a very difficult but must be done eventually. It is best to really weigh both options and go with our intuition. In this card you can see that both swords are exactly the same in appearance. The Two of Swords can also represent making a decision between two equally weighted options that have been nagging at us for a while. This card can represent that moment of relief just after we've decided between the two options. There is still a level of grieving, however, for the option we didn't choose. Are you using your gut in weighing these options?

When reversed, the Two of Swords usually indicates that we are struggling to choose between two options that both have negative consequences. Now especially it is extra important that we lay out all the pros and cons of both options so we can make the most informed decision. What is your intuition telling you about these decisions? What future changes could each option bring?

THREE OF SWORDS

The Three of Swords can be a very painful card. It often represents heartbreak, separation, sorrow, broken relationships, loss,
and grieving. The Three of Swords also reminds us that pain
is a necessary part of life and a great tool for learning. It shows
us that without pain we wouldn't learn from our mistakes and

therefore grow. The rain in this card can symbolize the need for release. Just like the cloud finally releases its water, sometimes simply letting yourself release tears can help relieve the pressure that builds up in your mind. Do you fight painful emotions? Could you benefit from feeling your emotions instead of burying them? The Three of Swords is not always a negative card. When taken literally this card can simply represent getting down to the heart of the matter. That could be a painful process but it doesn't always have to be.

When reversed, the Three of Swords often indicates that the dark times are behind us. It can signify that we have worked through our difficulties and are back on track to reaching our goals. When reversed, however, this card can also indicate that we are having a hard time working through our current obstacle.

Four of Swords

The Four of Swords is a card of meditation and taking time to think about our situations and actions. It can also be simply taking time to rest after hard work. The card depicts a woman meditating over and "charging" her tools after a long battle. The Four of Swords is about letting us know that the hard times are coming to an end and we can let our guard down. In today's fast-paced world we often don't give ourselves the necessary time to slow down and relax. Unfortunately that can lead to burnout. It is important to let ourselves rest and recharge after a long hard road so we are better equipped for the obstacles ahead. This card can also indicate a need for seclusion. Overall the Four of Swords is about allowing ourselves a break. Where can you add a little down time into your life? Do you take time for yourself?

When reversed, the Four of Swords can indicate that we just aren't taking the break that our bodies so desperately need. It could mean that our minds are going a million miles an hour while our bodies are begging for rest. Taking time to meditate and calm our minds can give us that necessary time out.

FIVE OF SWORDS

In the Five of Swords we see a woman boastfully grinning with her swords after defeating the crumpled figure in the background. This card can signify a conflict or disagreement. However, the Five of Swords reminds us not to be too aggressive in our pursuits as a "winning at all costs" attitude can leave us worse off than we were before. We need to remember not to step on others to get what we want. The Five of Swords can also signify that we are being too passive and need to stand up for ourselves. Are you being bullied? Are you always being talked over at work? Now may be a good time to speak up and take a stand.

When reversed, the Five of Swords can indicate that we are ready to end any current conflicts; we just want to forgive and forget. It can represent that we are open and ready for change once all the conflict has been resolved. When reversed, however, the Five of Swords can also signify that there is leftover resentment after a conflict. Discussing that resentment with those involved may help move us forward.

Six of Swords

I have always equated the Six of Swords with crossing the river Styx in Greek mythology or with a Norse funeral, a transition from one stage of life to the next. As with any transition or change, there is a level of mourning our previous stage. The Six of Swords can also signify the need to move forward from a loss or death, which is where the Norse funeral comes into play. Paying our respects and truly honoring the loss in any way we are able help us move forward while still being respectful of the mourning process. The rough water on one side of the boat and the smooth calm water on the other side symbolize the need to transition from a negative and stressful situation into one much calmer and smooth. The Six of Swords can also be taken quite literally and simply mean a trip across water.

When reversed, the Six of Swords usually indicates that we are having a hard time with a transition or change. What about this change is scary? What can you do to make this transition easier for yourself? It is sometimes simply meditation and a little introspection that we need to help us figure out what is keeping us stuck to better understand how we can change it.

Seven of Swords

The Seven of Swords can have numerous meanings. It can sometimes be read as a warning from the thief who is trying to take something from us and add unnecessary stress. It can warn of betrayal and deceit from outside sources. Have you taken something that isn't yours? Are you or someone around you acting with intent to deceive? The Seven of Swords can also read as simply running away. Running away isn't always negative—if we are running away from a bad situation or from something that is no longer serving us, it can be the best thing for us. Could you benefit from getting away from your current situation quickly? The Seven of Swords can also indicate a desire to go out on our own.

When reversed, the Seven of Swords can indicate that we are running away but in a negative sense. Are you running away from your fears instead of facing them? Are you dealing with your problems or are you in denial? The Seven of Swords reversed can also indicate that we are growing tired of a deceitful way of life. Are you engaging in an affair or lying at work? Are you exhausted from keeping up the charade?

EIGHT OF SWORDS

The Eight of Swords is all about the tendency to hold ourselves back. The swords being a suit of thoughts, the woman being bound and surrounded by scattered swords shows that she is feeling trapped by her own perspective. When we look closer, however, we can see that directly behind her is a break in the swords and that she isn't really trapped. If she could just remove that blindfold she could see the reality. Could your thoughts and perspectives be limiting you? Are you feeling stuck? Could your own actions have led to the current situation? The Eight of Swords can also hint that you are going to be met with opposition from outside forces; you need to rediscover your power and trust your gut.

When reversed, the Eight of Swords indicates that we have been through some rough times but we aren't letting ourselves fall prey to those self-limiting thoughts we all possess. It reassures us that we are on the right path of moving forward and not letting ourselves get too stuck in the past. We are taking responsibility for our actions.

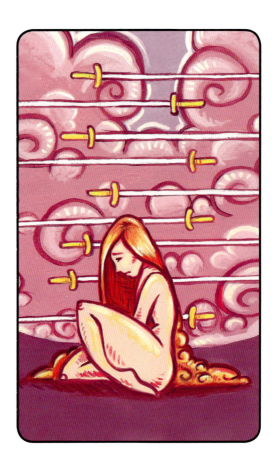

NINE OF SWORDS

The Nine of Swords is a card of internal despair and conflict. While the Ten of Swords is more about external factors, the Nine of Swords is all about how our minds can play tricks on our perspectives. This is a card of depression, anxiety, and fears. The wall of swords around the girl represents the wall we create when we fall prey to our fears and anxieties. Are you worrying excessively about something? Do your thoughts and worry keep you up at night? Are your inner voices negative or positive? The Nine of Swords reminds us that we are often too hard on ourselves. We can't let fear and worry immobilize us and need to remember that it can skew our perspective and make things seem much worse than they actually are. Take extra time for self-care and meditation to help solve your problem.

The Nine of Swords reversed can indicate that we are making a mountain out of a molehill or that we are being dramatic. Emotions can be very powerful but wallowing in them doesn't help anything. At some point we must move on and get back on track toward our goals. What baby steps can you take to get yourself unstuck?

Ten of Swords

The Ten of Swords has a very negative feel to it at first; her posture and the ten swords in her back are the first clues to these feelings. This card often speaks not only of a sudden loss, disaster, accident, betrayal, and backstabbing, but also of victimhood and playing the martyr. This card could indicate an event that just happened or is yet to occur. The Ten of Swords also reminds us of the importance of taking responsibility for our actions and not placing the entirety of the blame outside ourselves. The Ten of Swords reminds us that we need not focus too deeply on the negatives in our lives and focus more on what we can do to make it better. The sunrise behind her reminds us that there is always hope. This card is very similar to the Death card and can also signify a need for change or rebirth. What thoughts and beliefs have brought you here? Are you comforted by these self-limiting thoughts?

When reversed, the Ten of Swords can indicate that we are resisting an inevitable end or "death" of a situation in order to avoid pain. Resisting change will only add more pain and suffering. Like its upright counterpart, the reversed Ten of Swords reminds us that there is always hope and light even in the darkest situations. It also reminds us that these situations aren't usually nearly as bad as we imagine they will be.

PAGE OF SWORDS

The Page of Swords is a youthful card full of energy that centers mostly on communication. He is eager to begin his journey and ultimately discover life's truths for himself. He is very skilled at communication and uses that skill to uncover the truths around him. The Page of Swords likes to explore and discover new things. He urges us to ask questions of those around us so we can gain a better understanding of our current situations. He also often shines new light, bringing with him new ideas and messages. Because of his young age, however, the Page of Swords hasn't quite mastered how to tactfully suggest new ideas or inspirations and can become quite annoying to those around him. He also has the propensity to become somewhat of a gossip in his pursuit of knowledge. Do you recognize his energy in yourself or someone around you? How can recognizing these traits help you move forward?

When reversed, the Page of Swords indicates you or someone using communication skills to manipulate and deceive those around him. He may come across as a know-it-all and not really listen or pay attention to those around him. The reversed Page of Swords reminds us to not get too obsessed with the pursuit of truth and information. Keep the balance of also listening to those around you.

Knight of Swords

The Knight of Swords is a very headstrong card. He has a clear view of his goals and locks on target, completely blocking out any obstacles that may stand between him and those goals. He is very ambitious and confident but completely ignoring the risks can also come back to bite him in the future. The Knight of Swords represents the excitement in the beginning of a new project or situation. We have an initial burst of energy to get moving toward our goals, but we need to remind ourselves to not rush through things or skimp on the quality of the work. Just like the King and Queen, the Knight of Swords is very intelligent and rational, but he can be very impatient and jump to conclusions. Do you recognize these traits in yourself or someone in your life? How can they help you move forward?

When the reversed Knight of Swords comes up in a reading, he usually signifies an aspect of yourself or a person in your life who has no clear direction and is therefore all over the place. He lacks any real rational ideas and has a million grandiose plans; however, none of them will ever take flight. The reversed Knight of Swords can also indicate that we are moving too fast in our stage of life or situation and need to slow down and really pay attention to what is going on around us.

Queen of Swords

The Queen of Swords is a very strong, independent woman. Like her husband, she is level-headed, knowing what she wants and unafraid to go after it. She is stern and doesn't let her emotion cloud her judgment. The Queen of Swords makes very fair and impartial judgments, and she urges us to do the same in our situations. She can also be brutally honest. The Queen of Swords doesn't sugarcoat her messages. She tells us exactly what we need to hear regardless of how it will make us feel. Emulating these traits in our interactions with others and our selves may help us with our current situation. Could these traits represent yourself or someone around you? Could her energy benefit your current situation?

When reversed, the Queen of Swords is often trying to tell us that we are letting emotion cloud our judgment too much. She can also be indicating that emotional or outside forces are clouding our normally clear vision. What is currently distracting you? How can you work to clear those distractions to get back on track? The Queen of Swords reversed can also indicate that her bluntness is also being taken to a negative extreme.

King of Swords

The King of Swords is a very powerful, clear-thinking, and intellectual authority figure. He makes decisions with a very logical frame of mind. He holds true to his values and doesn't sway to peer pressure. The King of Swords urges us to solve our problems using fair judgment and logic while obeying the law. He does not let his emotions cloud his judgment. He often represents either an aspect of yourself that you need to recognize or a person in your life who could give you advice on your situation. Who could this card represent? How could the traits and energy of this card help your current situation?

The reversed King of Swords uses his intellect and authority to a negative extreme. He uses his intelligence to manipulate those around him for his own gain. This card urges us to cut out the people in our lives that exhibit these characteristics or to recognize them in ourselves so we can work to change them. When reversed The King of Swords can also be a sign that we are avoiding making decisions in an aspect of our lives. Have you been putting off any decisions?

Suit of Pentacles

The suit of pentacles is represented by the element earth. Green is the symbolic color of earth. This suit deals with material objects such as money and work. However, it also refers to our outward physical consciousness, like our health, and how we interact with the world around us. It represents manifestation, awareness, and accomplishment. The earth is filled with bountiful resources, and that is shown beautifully in this suit. Pentacles urge us to use our resources and each card will show the different ways we can create, shape, and make them work toward our goals. The negative aspects of this suit include greed, over-indulging, over-spending, and a materialistic attitude. Being tied to the earth element, the pentacles often remind us of the importance of nature and remaining grounded.

Ace of Pentacles

The Ace of Pentacles, like all the aces, is about new beginnings and the spark of new energy. This new energy brings with it a new wealth of opportunities and ideas for the taking. This card is about having a world of potential at our fingertips; however, we have to actually reach out and take the opportunities. The

Ace of Pentacles urges us to take that idea we've had on hold and finally make it a reality. It tells us to harness our energy now and make the most of it or we will lose it. Now is the time to start that new business or that new, healthy path of mental and physical self-care. Whatever our desires, this card urges us to make it happen. It is also an indicator for good health and or good fortune to come, however, we must work hard for it.

When reversed, the Ace of Pentacles urges us to be hesitant in starting any new projects or business ventures right now. It indicates that the timing may not be right for anything new. If we must begin a new project now, we are urged to take extra caution and plan carefully. It is probably best to hold off on the new project and focus more on making sure there is currently a healthy balance in our lives.

Two of Pentacles

The Two of Pentacles is about keeping balance while juggling all our responsibilities. The woman is dancing between two new business ideas and is concentrating on juggling them with all her other obligations. She works hard to keep everything in balance. As we can see by the look on her face, she takes this task very seriously—so seriously, in fact, that she doesn't see the storm brewing around her. This card reminds us to not get so swept up in our new ideas that we ignore and neglect everything else we have already worked for. It is a grounding card that urges us to carefully balance the old and the new in our lives. It also sometimes predicts change so it reminds us to stay flexible especially in the near future. Do you work to retain balance as new opportunities come along? Do you feel overwhelmed?

When reversed, the Two of Pentacles can indicate an inability to handle all of our day-to-day responsibilities. We aren't maintaining a proper balance between everything we find important; something or someone is getting neglected. This card shows us that we need to identify what we are neglecting and better manage our time to reincorporate it into our life.

THREE OF PENTACLES

The Three of Pentacles speaks of working together and collaborating with others to fulfill our goals. It also often indicates a passing of information from one generation to the next. The card shows a son showing his proud father that he has been working to take over where the father has stopped. This card represents encouragement to work together using all of our strengths to perfect and fulfill an overarching goal. The Three of Pentacles also draws on the importance of good communication and listening to constructive feedback from our peers and educators. Through support and working together, we can work harder and more efficiently toward our goal. Can working together help accomplish your goal faster? Do you take constructive criticism to heart?

When reversed, the Three of Pentacles can represent not working well in a group. There may be a lack of communication leading to added tension and confusion. This may be a sign to break free from this group and work independently. The reversed Three of Pentacles can also indicate a familial pressure to take on a business or project we don't really want. Communicating with the source of the pressure honestly and coming to a compromise may benefit our current situation.

Four of Pentacles

The Four of Pentacles is very conservative and controlling when it comes to money. This card indicates a very successful and financially secure person, who has grown his fortune through hard work and perseverance. Unfortunately, he also tends to be very conservative and stingy with his money—he clings to it desperately and doesn't let it out of his sight. He doesn't do this with purposeful malice, but fear. The Four of Pentacles reminds us in those moments to be gentle with those reacting in fear. It also reminds us not to let ourselves fall victim to fear and to retain the necessary balance between working toward our goals and enjoying the rewards. How has hoarding your resources felt beneficial? Could it be doing more harm than good? How do you feel about giving to others? What are your fears related to philanthropy?

The reversed Four of Pentacles can represent someone overspending their money and racking up large amounts of debt. They may have complete disregard for their future and are acting recklessly with money or possibly their health. It is important to keep the balance and keep our future in mind when planning. This card reversed can also indicate an obsessive need for control. It reminds us to occasionally let go of our need for security and control to relieve unnecessary stress and burden in our lives.

Five of Pentacles

The Five of Pentacles is a card of loss and poverty. This could be a loss in financial aspects or health aspects in our lives. This card sometimes indicates a feeling of shock and suddenly being left out in the cold. The Five of Pentacles also often indicates a period of suffering, either mentally or physically. It can indicate a feeling of isolation, abandonment, and depression, in that we feel like we are outside of our lives looking in. The Five of Pentacles urges us to reconnect with our support systems, ask for help where necessary, and be kind to ourselves as we work to rebuild our mental or physical lives. Do you feel lost? How can you seek help and get yourself back on track?

When reversed, this card also reminds us to keep our heads up in the face of adversity and stay humble in every aspect of our lives because we can very quickly fall from grace. It is the loss in this card that reminds the Six of Pentacles to help those who are in need. The Five of Pentacles reversed can also indicate a reconnection with our spiritual selves, as the stained glass window is popularly depicted as a church window. Do you feel connected with your faith? How can you regain that connection?

Six of Pentacles

The Six of Pentacles is a card of generosity, caring, and sharing the wealth. A very wealthy man travels the streets and generously gives to those less fortunate. His scales indicate that he is very fair and balanced when it comes to his charity, and he tries his best to help all he can equally. He doesn't give to others out of status or image; he truly cares about others and wishes them the best from the bottom of his heart. This card urges us to remember those who helped us in our own success and to pass that good energy along to others. It also reminds us that there is no shame in accepting others' charity when we really need it. Just remember to pay back others later on when you can. How do you feel about giving and receiving charity? Are you generous with your resources?

When reversed, the Six of Pentacles can represent giving but not out of the goodness of our hearts, rather only to further our own status and to bring more attention to ourselves. It can also be an indication of mounting debt. We may be acting recklessly with our spending or borrowing money with no means to pay back the loans. This card reminds us to be mindful of what we do with our money as it can really affect the future.

Seven of Pentacles

The Seven of Pentacles is about perseverance, time investment, and reward. This card depicts a young worker in the field taking a break to enjoy the fruits of his labor finally appearing. The Seven of Pentacles is a good omen that we will begin to see the rewards from all of our recent hard work. Invest time and effort now to ensure a fruitful and secure future. It is also a reassurance in frustrating times that our hard work really is going to pay off, and we shouldn't give up due to recent obstacles. The Seven of Pentacles also asks us to reassess if our rewards are worth all the hard work we put into it. How do you feel about growth? Is it time to take a break? Do you give yourself the appreciation you deserve?

When reversed, the Seven of Pentacles can indicate that we aren't investing the proper time and skill needed to see our goals come to life, or perhaps all of our hard work isn't going to pay off as hoped. It can also illuminate a feeling of instability in an aspect of our lives for which we'd worked really hard. It may be a time to really consider those feelings and decide if they are based in fear or reality, and what to do to rectify them.

Eight of Pentacles

The Eight of Pentacles is a card about the actual process of learning and harnessing a new skill. This card embodies the idea that practice makes perfect. We see a young man perfecting his craft by practicing over and over again. The monotonous and repetitious work is one of the most important factors in improving a new skill. We don't become masters overnight, rather only through tedious hard work. The Eight of Pentacles acts as encouragement to persist in our current tasks as eventually it is going to pay off. This card represents the importance of continuing to put effort into bettering ourselves, be it in a new skill or in general in our overall lives. Do you enjoy what you do? Does it come naturally to you? What drives you to work so hard?

Reversed, the Eight of Pentacles can represent an obsessive level of perfectionism that is hindering our ability to move forward on our path. There must be a balance to do our best but also not get so stuck in the process honing our craft that we are unable to do anything else. It can also indicate that the project we are currently working very hard on may not have the outcome we had hoped for. It may be a time to reevaluate our plans.

NINE OF PENTACLES

The Nine of Pentacles represents self-sufficiency and independence. A woman walks alone in her vast garden, reflecting on all of her wealth and knowledge. The taming of the wild falcon on her arm suggests a strong self-control over her spiritual and intellectual self. She is independent and strong and doesn't rely on anyone else for her stability and security in life. She is refined and ladylike while enjoying the worldly pleasures she worked hard to earn. The Nine of Pentacles is close to the end of her business path; however, she has one last obstacle or stage before she reaches the complete fulfillment we see in the Ten of Pentacles. This card can act as a reminder to not rest quite yet, as there is a bit more left to go on this path. Do your goals allow personal growth? How can you bring more balance to better reach your goals?

When reversed, the Nine of Pentacles can indicate a need to let go of a certain ideal image we have set for our home and ourselves. Sometimes we lose ourselves in a constant struggle to keep up with the ideal image of society around us. No one is perfect, and letting go of the need to constantly prove ourselves to everyone else can release a huge amount of energy better put to use elsewhere.

TEN OF PENTACLES

The Ten of Pentacles represents completion and fulfillment of our goals. We are shown an old man who has worked hard for his money and is finally retiring so he can enjoy it. He now gets to share his wealth with his family and loved ones, enjoying all the worldly pleasures that money can buy. This man has reached the stage of ultimate stability and prosperity in his life and now seeks to teach others about what he has learned. The Ten of Pentacles can urge us to actually enjoy our wealth and not simply save it, never to be used. It wants us to be grateful for what we have and to share our fortune with those around us. How can you benefit those around you? Are you a little tight-fisted with your money? Now that you've retired in this current stage, what's next?

When reversed, the Ten of Pentacles can represent smug-ness and greed. It can speak of hoarding our fortunes, and boast-ing about our fortunes with an unwillingness to share with our loved ones around us. It can also indicate a failure to plan and se-cure that financial foundation in our life. Perhaps we didn't plan for our future and are lacking that stability. Let this card serve as a reminder to keep our future financial needs in mind as we make our business plans.

Page of Pentacles

The Page of Pentacles is young and eager to learn and manifest goals into reality. Like all pages, this one is full of ideas and eager energy, but he is especially is driven by money. This card urges us to learn new skills in order to be successful later on in life. The Page of Pentacles represents that young soul in our lives who is an entrepreneur at heart. Business sense just comes naturally to him and he is constantly eager to start new business projects. This card urges us to learn as much as we can in our business field to ensure our success. It can also represent starting over in a new career regardless of age.

When reversed, the Page of Pentacles can represent a lack of success due to insufficient planning or not being willing to put in the necessary work. It can also indicate that we are getting into a new project for the wrong reasons, perhaps simply for the money. If we don't have the passion for a field and profession, we may burn out quickly and not reach our goals.

KNIGHT OF PENTACLES

The Knight of Pentacles is very smart and successful but very particular and a bit slow in his processes. Speaking for myself, he has always come across as a bit of a nerdy character (not "nerdy" in the negative sense, simply a descriptor of his processes). He is methodical and a bit of a perfectionist when it comes to his work. The Knight of Pentacles is young but very intelligent. He can solve most problems put in front of him through tinkering and exploration and has had great success in business because of this. He is seen as very trustworthy and always willing to help. This knight is often seen as a bit boring, and indeed this card can represent the mundane everyday activities in daily life when not referring to an actual person or aspect of ourselves. Do you recognize these traits in yourself or someone around you?

When reversed, the Knight of Pentacles can represent feeling stuck in the everyday grind. It can represent feeling bored and restless with our current situations. This card reversed reminds us to mix things up occasionally to break free from that repetition. It can also indicate a person who has taken perfectionism to an extreme such that it is affecting their life or the lives of those around them.

Queen of Pentacles

The Queen of Pentacles is an earthy woman and mother. She is an avid gardener and loves spending time engulfed in nature. The Queen of Pentacles nurtures growth within us in all aspects of our lives, but most specifically she creates a warm comforting home filled with all the love and support we need.

She represents security and prosperity, and teaches by example. She urges us to grow our business with loving, caring, and compassionate energy. The Queen of Pentacles urges us to keep the balance between family and business, and reminds us to take the time to use our wealth to help and enjoy our loved ones around us. Could harnessing these traits benefit you in your current situation?

When reversed, the Queen of Pentacles can represent spending so much time obsessed with work and success that we are neglecting our loved ones and perhaps our own mental health. The reminder is to keep the balance between business and other aspects of our lives. The Queen of Pentacles reversed can also refer to a tendency to smother others with our love instead of simply mothering them. It is important to let others be independent and trust that they will take the lessons you taught them to heart on their own.

KING OF PENTACLES

The King of Pentacles is a king of abundance, wealth, wisdom, and control. He can represent the final successful stage of a task. Like all kings, he is a father figure full of wisdom, but this one is particularly smart when it comes to money and finances. He personifies financial stability. The King has worked hard for his riches and likes to show them off. His people look up to and respect him. The King of Pentacles is also about hard work and discipline. He keeps a strict and tight level of control over his finances and his business. When not referring to a person, the King of Pentacles urges us to manage our tasks with precision and care to ensure a successful final result. He speaks of taking the path well travelled to protect our wealth. How can these traits benefit you now? Do you see his energy in yourself or someone around you?

When reversed, the King of Pentacles can indicate an obsession with material things. Perhaps we are getting too caught up in a lavish lifestyle in hopes of finding happiness. It may also indicate that we are becoming so preoccupied with the pursuit of money that other aspects of our lives are suffering. The King of Pentacles reversed can serve as a reminder that there are many more important aspects to life, such as family.

Conclusion

The most important point I want you to take away from this book is that tarot is wholly personal. It shouldn't be scary or intimidating. There are hundreds of different ways to interpret the cards, but what matters most is finding what works for you or changing the rules and making it your own. The cards simply tap into to our own deep-seated human characteristics and use our own intuition to help shine a light on the aspects of our lives that we may not be consciously aware of. The Vivid Journey deck uses traditional Rider-Waite-Smith imagery and color to help intensify that intuitive connection. I poured my own energies into each image to create flowing lines of color.

My hope is that with all of these elements, you are better able to deepen your connection with tarot. I aim to make it a little easier to read the cards and illuminate your own personal journeys or the journeys of those for whom you are reading. I hope you enjoy the vivid imagery and find guidance on whatever path your journey takes you!